INTRODUCTION
Getting to know Guernsey

GUERNSEY

Vale

St Sampson • **ST SAMPSON**

HERM

Castel

ST PETER PORT

JETHOU

• L'ERÉE
St Peter
in the
Wood

St Savior

St Andrew

BRECQHOU

Torteval

✈ Forest

St Martin

N

0   10 km
0   6 miles

UNITED KINGDOM

ENGLISH CHANNEL

CHANNEL ISLANDS

ALDERNEY

GUERNSEY ◄ HERM

SARK

JERSEY

FRANCE

DONATION ~~Sp~~

CONTENTS

SYMBOLS KEY 4

INTRODUCTION 5

Map of the Channel Islands 6

Getting to know Guernsey 8

Map of Guernsey 14

The best of Guernsey 16

RESORTS 19

St Peter Port 20

St Sampson & Vale 26

Castel & St Saviour 30

St Peter in the wood
   & Torteval 33

Forest, St Martin
   & St Andrew 36

Herm 42

Sark 48

Alderney 54

EXCURSIONS 61

Bailiwick beach tour 62

Map of Jersey 66

St Helier, Jersey 68

Southern tour, Jersey 76

Northern tour, Jersey 86

St Ouen, Jersey 94

LIFESTYLE 97

Food & drink 98

Shopping 102

Kids 105

Festivals & events 108

Sports & activities 110

PRACTICAL INFORMATION 113

Preparing to go 114

During your stay 119

INDEX 125

ACKNOWLEDGEMENTS 128

SYMBOLS KEY

The following is a key to the symbols used throughout this book:

i information office   ✝ church   ▣ café

🚌 bus stop   ➘ tip   🍸 bar/pub

✉ post office   🛍 shopping   🏵 fine dining

✈ airport   🍴 restaurant

---

① telephone   **🅕** fax   **ⓔ** email   **ⓦ** website address

ⓐ address   **🕑** opening times   **❶** important

£ budget price   ££ mid-range price   £££ most expensive

★ specialist interest   ★★ see if passing   ★★★ top attraction

---

BURHOU

ST ANNE

ALDERNEY

THE ENGLISH CHANNEL

JERSEY

St Ouen

St John &
St Mary

ROZEL

St Peter

St Lawrence

St Martin
& Trinity

St Brelade

St Saviour

PULENTE

St Helier

GOREY

St Clement
& Grouville

ST HELIER

LA ROCQUE

Getting to know Guernsey

Guernsey island, along with Herm, Sark and Alderney, which together form the Bailiwick of Guernsey, attracts thousands of visitors every year, and it's easy to see why. All the islands have an extraordinary leisurely way of life, beautiful countryside and waterfront buildings, dramatic coastlines and bays, fabulous seafood and some of the friendliest people you will ever meet.

Finding Guernsey isn't easy on most maps. Drop a mental plumb-line due south of Weymouth, in Dorset, and you will find this chip of granite adrift somewhere west of Cherbourg – much closer to France than to the UK, and a good bit warmer and sunnier. On a European scale, Guernsey, and even more so Herm, Sark and Alderney, look minute, but size isn't everything. In fact, the small scale of this seductive archipelago is all part of the charm factor.

The islands, along with their close Channel Island neighbour, Jersey, are all subtly different destinations, which serve up a tantalising variety of flavours. After sampling one, you may find yourself returning for another taste. You can easily have more than one plateful in a single trip: island-hopping is no problem.

So whether you want extraordinary landscapes and coastline, heritage, educational family fun and above all peace, Guernsey, Herm, Sark and Alderney have the lot. Top this off with duty-free shopping (there's no VAT in Guernsey) and some particularly fine dining and the contentment is complete.

GUERNSEY

Guernsey is the second largest of the Channel Islands after Jersey. Although densely populated, it feels quiet and intimate. It has stacks of charm, especially along its pretty, cliff-fringed southern coastline and in its delightful capital, St Peter Port. Excellent historic sights, shops and craft centres throughout the island add to its attractions. It even has its own little island, Lihou, which is an absolute haven of peace and an

◆ *Guernsey's coastline is rugged and beautiful*

important conservation area. The island was purchased by the States of Guernsey in January 1995. Visitors to Guernsey island can cross a causeway from the L'Erée headland at low water to reach it – but always check the tide tables before doing so, because at this point, the tide comes in at an alarming rate.

GUERNSEY TOWNS

St Peter Port is the hub of life on Guernsey island. A cosmopolitan harbour town typified by its historic buildings, cobbled streets and a marina with yachts gently rocking in the swell, it offers sophisticated family fun, superb shopping and fine dining.

Guernsey itself has a number of parishes, each with their own character. St Sampson is the industrial heart of the island, while Vale, Castel and St Saviour have some of the finest beaches and headlands. St Peter in the Wood and Torteval revel in dramatic coastlines, but the parishes of Forest and St Martin tend to have more sheltered bays and beaches, making them ideal for novice swimmers. Inland, St Andrews has outstanding countryside.

The islands of Herm, Sark and Alderney each offer a different look on life, and can be reached by ferry, hovercraft or, in some cases, helicopter or light aircraft. Lihou Island, a great place to unwind that lies just off the L'Erée headland on Guernsey, can be reached by a causeway.

1066 AND ALL THAT...

The French call the Channel Islands 'Les Isles Anglo-Normandes'. They once formed part of the Duchy of Normandy, and passed into English hands with William the Conqueror. When King John lost control of his Norman possessions in 1204, the Channel Islands were given the choice of reverting to France or remaining English. Shrewdly, they opted for the English side, on condition that they retained their own government and their ancient feudal privileges, relics of which they still hold today.

Thus the Channel Islands are British Isles, but they are not part of the United Kingdom. They have their own government and culture, their own laws and customs – even their own currency, postal services and tax systems. They bear allegiance to the Crown, but not to Westminster. Nor to Brussels either – the Channel Islands are not full members of the EU. For the Channel Islanders, the British monarch is still the Duke of Normandy, and when they drink a loyal toast, they raise their glasses to 'The Queen, Our Duke'. But age-old rivalries still exist between the islands, especially between Jersey and Guernsey – each took separate sides in the English Civil War (1642).

SEIGNEURS AND DAMES

The Norman feudal system, in which parcels of land were granted by the king in exchange for military service, has long since lapsed on the larger islands. But some of the ancient manor houses remain, and a few are still inhabited by descendants of the original seigneurial families, such as Sausmarez Manor on Guernsey, or St Ouen's Manor on neighbouring Jersey. You can visit both of these, and find out more. Sark tantalises political historians as the last remaining feudal society in Europe, still with its Seigneur or Dame as ruler, in name if not in practice. By one of those odd paradoxes so typical of the Channel Islands, however, it was never actually feudal in feudal times. Its seigneurial system dates only from 1565.

BEATING THE TAXMAN

Low taxation makes Guernsey, Alderney, Sark and Herm, plus their neighbouring island of Jersey, extremely attractive for wealthy settlers; there's always a long queue of millionaires on the waiting list. If you win the lottery next week and decide to become a tax exile, you may find resident status is an elusive and protracted goal. For holiday visitors, though, the lower costs of some items, especially jewellery, alcohol, car hire and petrol, give the islands that extra sparkle.

HERM

Herm is tiny (less than a square mile in area) with gorgeous beaches and a charmingly rural interior. Its appeal far outweighs its diminutive size and many devotees find the absence of contrived amusements a distinct advantage. Under the careful supervision of its tenant managers, it promises a tranquil, civilized retreat for a day-trip – or longer.

SARK

Sark, similarly, has glorious scenery and its winsome feudal customs make it an instant hit with visitors. You can easily see it on a day trip, as thousands do, but it is even better if you stay at one of its excellent hotel-restaurants. There are two privately owned islands in these waters too. **Jethou** is off the coast of Herm and **Brecqhou** is at Sark, although these can't be visited – unless you're invited.

ALDERNEY

Alderney is the third largest of the Channel Islands and is a self-govern-ing, democratic territory. It is less populous than Guernsey and lies around 37 km (23 miles) north east of the island. Its geography keeps it free of mass tourism so it has a special appeal for lovers of peace and quiet, bird-watching and open spaces. Its coastline, fringed by fortresses, sandy beaches and rugged cliffs, is uniquely memorable.

THE OTHER CHANNEL ISLAND – JERSEY

Jersey is the big one, 14 km (9 miles) across at its widest, basking in southerly sunshine like a glamorous bathing belle. It's a wealthy place, and its residents enjoy the good life in smart restaurants and yacht marinas. Well endowed with superb beaches and high-profile tourist attractions, it has a surprising amount of unspoilt rural scenery too, criss-crossed by a web of tiny lanes. Jersey has more organised entertain-ment and nightlife than the other islands (see Excursions, pages 66–96).

 Herm is proud of its Shell Beach

THE ENGLISH CHANNEL

N

0   2 km
0   1 mile

Saline Bay

Cobo Bay

COBO

ALBECQ

Vazon Bay

Perelle Bay

LE GELÉ

LIHOU ISLAND

Le Tricoteur • MONT SAINT

GUER

CASTEL

ERÉE

L'Erée Bay

ST SAVIOUR

LES BUTTES

Rocquaine Bay

ST PETER IN THE WOOD

Guernsey Woodcarvers • Strawberry Farm

Fort Grey

Guernsey Coppercraft

Coach House Gallery

LA VILLIAZ

Portelet Bay

Le Coudré

LONGFIRE

Bruce Russell

PLEINMONT

TORTEVAL PARISH CHURCH

ST PIERRE DUBOIS CHURCH

LES LANDES

LA BOURG

TORTEVAL

Hougue Anthan

TORTEVAL

German Occupation Museum

LES LAURENS

FOREST

Pembroke &
L'Ancrese
Bays

Fort Doyle

Beaucette
Marina

Fontanelle Bay

Ladies
Bay

LA FONTENELLE

Rousse Tower • Le Grande
Havre

VALE

VALE PARISH
CHURCH

Pétils Bay

LA PASÉE

tinfer
Bay

L'ISLET

BORDEAUX

Bordeaux
Harbour

RANDES
OCQUES

LES MARTINS

• Guernsey
Freesia Centre

• Vale Castle

• Oatlands Village

VINGTAINE
DE L'EPINE

• Guernsey
Candles

ST SAMPSON

ST SAMPSON
PARISH CHURCH

ST SAMPSON

Saumarez Park &
• Folk Museum

Belle Grève Bay

• Telephone Museum

VILLOQUE

LAES VARENDES

STEL PARISH
CHURCH

ST PETER
PORT

EY

Priaulx
Library

LA MONNAIE

TOWN CHURCH

• Castle Cornet

Havelet Bay

BAILIFFS CROSS

La Valette
Underground
Military Museum

ST ANDREW

ST ANDREW'S
PARISH CHURH

• Catherine
Best Studio

Soldier's Bay

Little Chapel

German
Underground
Hospital

LA GRAN'MERE
DU CHIMQUIÈRE

ST MARTINS
PARISH CHURCH

• La Gran'mère
du Chimquière

• Sausmarez
Manor

Fermain Bay

LES NICOLLES

ST MARTIN

VILETTE

• Moulin Huet
Pottery

Le Pied du Mur
(Marble Bay)

Petie
Bot Bay

Saint's
Bay

Moulin
Huet
Bay

Petit
Port

• Le Pied du
Jerbourg Gardens

Icart

◆ *St Martin's Church*

The best of Guernsey

CHURCHES

Each of the parishes of Guernsey has its own church. Many of them are handsome and surprisingly large buildings – interesting inside and out. The smaller islands also have churches worth visiting. Below is a short list of some you may like to see if you're passing. Many have interesting modern stained glass – St Saviour's is especially intriguing.

- **St Peter's Church** The Town Church in St Peter Port is full of interesting monuments. Look out for the Ten Commandments, which are written in Norman French on the altar (see page 20).
- **St Saviour's Church** The parish church of St Saviour is one of the largest on Guernsey, with lovely stained glass (see page 30).
- **St Martin's Church** A fascinating church, famous for the monument its the gate (see pages 18 and 39).

CASTLES & FORTRESSES

For over a thousand years the Channel Islands have been subjected to invasion, or threats of invasion. All around the coastline, the islanders have tried to ward off the danger by building fortresses and watch-towers. Among the islands' best are:

- **Castle Cornet** A 13th-century waterfront fortress, Castle Cornet is a landmark on Guernsey. It contains historical, maritime and military museums (see page 20).
- **Rousse Tower** A mighty fortification on the headland just east of Le Grande Havre, Guernsey (see page 26).
- **Pleinmont Observation Tower** A five-story naval observation tower used by the Germans in 1942–45 (see page 33).
- **Fort Grey** This Martello tower at Rocquaine Bay contains the fascinating Shipwreck Museum, showing the perils of Guernsey's reef-strewn west coast (see page 34).
- **Fort Clonque, Alderney** A Victorian fort at the end of a concrete causeway (see page 56).

Guernsey also boasts the fascinating **La Gran'mère du Chimquière**, a Bronze Age curiosity which stands by the gate of St Martin's parish church and is well worth a visit. It depicts a female figure who is believed to have magical powers and, even today, flower garlands are placed on her head, especially after wedding ceremonies.

BEACHES
It is a well-known fact that Guernsey and its neighbouring islands possess some of the world's most beautiful and unspoilt beaches and bays. For a tour of the best of these, see Bailiwick beach tour, on page 62.

WORLD WAR II
World War II is an unforgettable period in Guernsey's history, as it, along with its neighbouring islands, was the only part of the British Isles to be invaded by the Germans. The Occupation Story is told in two museums on the island, and visitors often find them fascinating. Don't forget to look at the liberation monuments as well. You'll find Guernsey has an imaginative and very moving monument in St Peter Port (near the Clock Tower by the harbour), where the first German bombs fell in 1940. The best places to find out more are:

- **German Occupation Museum** Situated close to Le Bourg in the south, the museum recounts Guernsey's period of Occupation with authentic displays of World War II memorabilia (see page 36).
- **La Valette Underground Military Museum** Housed in a series of German wartime tunnels, this award-winning display of Occupation memorabilia is particularly atmospheric (see page 23).

Try to plan your itinerary so you see **La Coupée** on Sark (see also pages 48 and 50). A breathtaking neck of rock links Little Sark to the main island of Sark and is just wide enough for a tractor or horse and cart. It has dizzying drops to either side.

RESORTS
Places under the sun

St Peter Port
on the waterfront

In any Channel Island town beauty contest, Guernsey's St Peter Port wins hands down. The whole place focuses on the reclaimed waterfront. Ferries and fishing boats chug purposefully between the bristling jetties, while the halyards of the leisure boats clank in the breeze.

From the sea, St Peter Port's townscape of tall granite houses rising against wooded hillsides seems enmeshed in a cat's cradle of masts and maritime rigging. Exploring the picturesque old town takes you through steep cobbled streets linked by flights of steps, with plenty of good shops along the route, as well as the fascinating **Town Church**.

There's a lively cultural feel to St Peter Port too, with theatre and music venues as well as local craft centres and art galleries to visit. Don't forget to seek out Victor Hugo's home, the fascinating **Hauteville House**.

St Peter Port is the hub of life on Guernsey, so it's fitting that one of the island's largest community projects of recent years is on view here. **The Bailiwick of Guernsey Tapestry** is housed in a purpose built gallery in the Dorey Centre, next to the 19th-century church of St James the Less. Made by residents of Guernsey as a Millennium project, the tapestry comprises panels covering a century each, which collectively tell of 1,000 years of local history. It is well worth seeing if visiting St Peter Port.

THINGS TO SEE & DO
Castle Cornet ★★★
A major land and seamark, the 13th-century waterfront fortress contains historical, maritime and military museums. Constructed in King John's reign, it was last used for defensive purposes by the Germans in World War II. At midday, red-coated retainers fire an artillery salute from the Royal Battery. Get your camera ready. ➌ Castle Emplacement ➊ 01481 726 518 ➍ Open 10.00–17.00 (April–Oct) ➊ Admission charge

---

▶ St Peter Port's waterfront

THE ENGLISH CHANNEL

North Beach Marina

St Julian's Pier

The Harbour

Castle Cornet

Havelet Bay

German Naval HQ

Beau Séjour Leisure Centre

Guernsey Museum & Art Gallery

The Bailiwick of Guernsey Tapestry
St James Concert Hall

General Post Office

Town Church

Guernsey Toys

Victorian Shop and Parlour

La Mallard Hotel

Hauteville House (Victor Hugo's Home)

La Valette Underground Military Museum

Guernsey Aquarium

Castle Pier

N

0   100 m   250 m
0   600 ft

Guernsey Museum & Art Gallery ★★★

An excellent introduction to the history and activities of the island from Neolithic times. Audio-visual show and art gallery. Notice the pretty Victorian bandstand and Victor Hugo's statue in the surrounding park.
ⓐ Candie Gardens ☎ 01481 726 518 🕐 Open 10.00–17.00 (summer), 10.00–16.00 (winter) ❶ Admission charge

La Valette Underground Military Museum ★★

Housed in a series of German wartime tunnels, this award-winning display of Occupation memorabilia is particularly atmospheric and worth a visit.
ⓐ La Valette ☎ 01481 722 300 🕐 Open 10.00–17.00 (summer)
❶ Admission charge

Hauteville House (Victor Hugo's home) ★★

The French writer lived as a political refugee in St Peter Port during 1855–70, when he wrote his epic novel, *Les Miserables*. His astonishing taste in interior decor shows a resourceful streak. ⓐ Hauteville
☎ 01481 721 911 🕐 Open Mon–Sat noon–16.00 (April), Mon–Sat 10.00–16.00 (May–Sept); tours (45 mins) ❶ Admission charge

An excellent-value combined entrance ticket is available for three of Guernsey's most interesting historic sights: Castle Cornet, Guernsey Museum and Fort Grey.

RESTAURANTS & PUBS (see map opposite)

Absolute End ££ ❶ Award-winning seafood cooking on the seafront. Good-value set lunches. Attentive, polished service.
ⓐ Longstore, just north of St Peter Port ☎ 01481 723 822 🕐 Open for lunch and evening meals (times vary in winter)

Christie's ££ ❷ Stylish brasserie in the old town, overlooking the waterfront. Ideal for coffee and cakes, an early-evening drink, or a full meal. Live jazz most evenings. ⓐ Le Pollet ☎ 01481 726 624
🕐 Open for breakfast, snacks, lunch and dinner

23

Da Nello ££ ❸ Intimate candlelit dining room offering classic Italian cooking and plenty of seafood, charcoal grills and pastas. Courteous, practiced service. ⓐ 46 Lower Pollet ❶ 01481 721 552 ❶ Open for lunch and evening meals

Dix-Neuf Brasserie ££ ❹ Urbane bar-cum-brasserie in a modern setting. Young friendly staff and lively music. Everything from chic Mediterranean specials to English breakfasts or sticky toffee pudding, but pleasant just for a drink too. ⓐ 19 Commercial Arcade ❶ 01481 723 455 ❶ Open daily (winter times can vary)

Duke of Normandie £ ❺ Attractively renovated 18th-century hotel-pub offering a good range of wines and bar lunches in a nostalgic maritime setting with oak beams and roaring fires. Courtyard barbecue. ⓐ Lefevre Street ❶ 01481 721 431 ❶ Open for lunch and evening meals

La Frégate £££ ❻ For a special treat, book a table in this elegant hotel-restaurant at the top of the town, with panoramic views and memorable French cuisine. ⓐ Les Cotils ❶ 01481 724 624 ❶ Open for lunch and evening meals ❶ Smart dress required

Moore's Patisserie £ ❼ Try this civilised place for a break from shopping or sightseeing, set in smartly refurbished surroundings in a historic old-town building. Luscious Austrian-style pastries or healthy light lunches. On the same premises, try the cosy **Library Bar** for a drink or a carvery lunch. ⓐ Le Pollet ❶ 01481 724 452 ❶ Open for lunch and early evening meals

Pelican's Café £ ❽ Streamlined modern decor and friendly service characterize this spotless central coffee shop serving unpretentious fare with a touch of sophistication. ⓐ 24 Le Pollet ❶ 01481 713 636 ❶ Open Mon–Sat for breakfast, coffee, lunch and afternoon tea ❶ No smoking; credit cards not accepted

SHOPPING

Shopping in St Peter Port is a delight. Waterfront stores cater for visiting yachtsmen, while shops in the steep cobbled streets behind display a mouthwatering VAT-free range of classy clothes, jewellery, photographic equipment, electrical goods, perfumes and shoes.

If you have children to amuse, be sure to visit the National Trust's quaint **Victorian shop and parlour** (📍 26 Cornet Street) where costumed ladies sell sweets in jars, or **Guernsey Toys** (📍 Victoria Road) for a genuine Guernsey teddy. Philatelists should head for the **General Post Office** (📍 Smith Street) to see a free exhibition of Guernsey stamps and postal paraphernalia, with some special presentation packs on sale.

If antiques interest you, stroll up **Mill Street** and **Mansell Street**, lined with bygones and bric-a-brac, and tempting collectables.

NIGHTLIFE

Nightlife on Guernsey is relatively quiet. Local licensing laws permit pubs to open Monday–Saturday 10.00–23.45, Sundays noon–15.00 and 18.00–23.00. There are two cinemas, one in St Peter Port's **Beau Séjour Leisure Centre** and a multi-screen complex at **La Mallard Hotel** near the airport. Beau Séjour also stages drama productions in summer. The **St James Concert Hall** (a converted church in St Peter Port) hosts a range of concerts and other cultural events – details are available from the tourist office or at your hotel. For later and racier nightlife, try the nightclubs located on **Le Pollet** in the centre of town.

St Sampson & Vale
island powerhouse

The northern tip of Guernsey is low-lying and peaceful, despite being quite densely populated (in parts at least). Much land lies under greenhouse glass, or water catchment systems. Here, too, is Guernsey's only significant industrial centre, St Sampson. The cranes and warehouses of the island's main cargo port and the power station's fuming chimneys don't often feature on Guernsey's picture postcards, but if you like ports or industrial archaeology you may appreciate St Sampson's gritty authenticity. It has some useful, reasonably priced shops too.

For those who appreciate a look into a more distant past, several Neolithic sites have been discovered in nearby Vale, Guernsey's northernmost parish. Les Fouillages (small burial chambers) were unearthed on the golf course on **L'Ancresse Common** in 1978. Amateur archaeologists may also like to track down the megalithic dolmens (passage graves) of La Varde and Dehus.

Tucked into a sheltered rock basin on the island's northeast tip is Beaucette Marina, full of classy looking ocean-going yachts. If you enjoy walking, follow the coastal headlands – marvellous sites for migrant birds in spring and autumn. Castles and towers stud the headlands at every turn – **Vale Castle**, **Rousse Tower** and **Fort Doyle** are some of the most impressive. Large stretches of sand and reefs lie exposed at low tide, especially in L'Ancresse Bay or around Grand Havre. L'Ancresse Common is a gorse-covered stretch of moor and pastureland dotted with pine trees and placid tethered cattle. For further details on the beaches in the area, see Excursions on page 62.

If you're an active sort, try the go-kart track just north of St Peter Port, or the windsurfing centres at **Cobo** and **L'Ancresse Bays**. Fishing and diving expeditions can also be arranged. Swimmers should be careful on these coasts – even the sheltered eastern side has deceptive currents.

● *Loop Holed Tower at L'Ancresse Common*

THINGS TO SEE & DO
Guernsey Freesia Centre ★
For an insight into Guernsey's blooming mail-order flower business,
visit these fragrant glasshouses to watch planting, picking and packing.
ⓐ Route Carré, St Sampson ① 01481 248 185 ⓛ Open 09.00–17.00
ⓘ Admission free

Oatlands Craft Centre ★★

This former brickworks houses a complex of craft studios and gift shops: glass blowing, pottery, silverwork and knitwear are just some of the things on show. ⓐ Braye Road, St Sampson ☏ 01481 244 282 ⏰ Open 09.30–17.00 ⓘ Admission free

RESTAURANTS

Good daytime restaurants in northern Guernsey are thin on the ground, although it isn't difficult to get a snack. You may prefer to stock up with picnic provisions or fish and chips and find a quiet beach somewhere.

The Courtyard Brasserie ££ Located at Oatlands, this a la carte restaurant has a terrace overlooking the gardens and grounds. Dine in the large conservatory where teas and light lunches are available. The evening menu has achieved special recognition on the island with many awards for excellence . In addition vegetarian dishes and a full children's menu are available. ⓐ Oatlands Village, St Sampson ☏ 01481 249 525 ⏰ Open noon–14.30 and 17.30–21.30

Fryer Tuck's Halfway Cafe £ More than just a fish-and-chip shop, this unassuming seafront café offers sit-down meals with salmon and steaks as well as traditional takeaways, all at rock-bottom prices. ⓐ 1 Commercial Place, St Sampson ☏ 01481 249 448 ⏰ Open Mon–Sat 06.30–14.15, Sun 09.00–14.15 ⓘ Licensed, with parking

Turkish Delight ££ This is a non smoking restaurant set in the centre of St Sampsons. Expect a meal full of flavour and colour using traditional cooking techniques, served up in sophisticated Turkish style surroundings. Specialities include kebabs, octopus salad and 'death by chocolate'. ⓐ Southside, St Sampson ☏ 01481 247 122 ⓔ turkish.delight@hotmail.com ⏰ Open noon–14.30 and 18.00–late

◀ *Saumarez Park is Guernsey's largest public park*

Castel & St Saviour
bays and beauty

**The parishes of Castel (also known as Catel) and St Saviour are domi-
nated by three glorious bays – Perelle Bay, Vazon Bay and Cobo Bay on
the north coast, the latter seamlessly becoming Saline Bay. Each beach
has its own distinctive characteristics. Perelle Bay is created within a
dramatic show of rocks with natural headlands either side, while Vazon
Bay is a massive stretch of beach – in fact the deepest if not the longest
expanse of sand on the island. Its width makes it a magnet with surfers
and sand-racers. Cobo Bay, with sand dunes hugging its north perime-
ter, is one of the prettiest bays, its belt of sand broken only by reefs.**

Inland of these three bays, you'll find rolling hills, sleepy lanes and quite
a few nature reserves – the island of Guernsey is home to more than
450 flowering plants and many of these can be seen in the Castel and
St Saviour parishes throughout the seasons. Don't miss the lovely
stained glass windows at St Saviour's parish church.

THINGS TO SEE & DO
Bruce Russell & Son: Gold, Silversmiths and Jewellers ★★
Watch skilled craftsfolk hand-finishing the elegant range of jewellery
and artefacts on sale in these 16th-century showrooms. Ancillary
attractions include immaculate gardens and the Furze Oven café.
⊜ Le Gron, St Saviour ❶ 01481 264 321 ❷ Open daily 09.00–17.00
(summer); closed Sun in winter ❶ Admission free

Saumarez Park & Folk Museum ★★★
Don't confuse this fine estate with St Martin's Sausmarez Manor,
owned by a separate (and differently spelled!) branch of the ancient
seigneurial family. Here, Guernsey's National Trust has set up a folk
museum, recreating typical period interiors. There are also nature trails,
a children's playground, tearooms and a shop. ❸ Castel ❶ 01481 255 384
❷ Open 10.00–17.30 (Easter–Oct) ❶ Admission charge

◐ *Sunset over the vast sandy expanse of Vazon bay*

Strawberry Farm ★★

This novel crop of over 50,000 strawberry plants in suspended growbags is also a tourist attraction, with gift and craft shops, play areas and tea gardens. ⊜ Les Issues, St Saviour ❶ 01481 268 015/264 428 ◕ Open 10.00–17.00 (Easter–Oct) ❶ Admission free

Le Tricoteur ★

Track down this knitwear factory in an old bakery near the coast at Perelle Bay, watch the production process, then check the prices of classic hand-finished Guernseys and other woollen and cotton goods. Children's and extra-large sizes available. ⊜ Perelle Bay ❶ 01481 264 040 ◕ Open Mon–Fri 08.30–17.00 and Sat 08.30–16.00 ❶ Admission free

Guernsey Woodcarvers ★★

Although under separate management, Guernsey Woodcarvers and Strawberry Farm can easily be seen on the same visit. The woodcarving studio produces a large range of attractive, portable souvenirs and furniture from over 60 types of timber. Watch skilled craftsmen turning, carving, French polishing, furniture-restoring and cabinet-making.
ⓐ Les Issues, St Saviour ⓣ 01481 265 373 ⓛ Open all year 09.00–17.00
ⓘ Admission free

RESTAURANTS

As in St Sampson and Vale, the selection of restaurants is somewhat limited. Of course, it is always possible to find a snack, but as in other towns in northern Guernsey, you may be better off having a picnic or finding tasty fish and chips for takeaway to enjoy by the sea. The following restaurants are worth a visit, however:

Cobo Bay Hotel ££ Ambitious combinations of sweet and savoury ingredients and lots of fresh fish are on the dinner menus in this agreeable seaside hotel. Ultra-attentive service and a good-value table d'hôte. ⓐ Cobo Bay, Castel ⓣ 01481 257 102 ⓛ Open daily

Fleur du Jardin ££ This charming farmhouse inn has achieved an enviable reputation for its food. Traditional bar food and more interesting restaurant fare with fresh fish, game and roasts. ⓐ King's Mills, Castel ⓣ 01481 257 996 ⓛ Open daily for lunch and evening meals ⓘ It is popular, so it is best to book ahead

Hougue du Pommier ££ Non-residents are welcome at this pleasant old farmhouse hotel near Cobo Bay, which features filling lunch or evening bar snacks, and full à la carte in the restaurant. ⓐ La Route de la Hougue du Pommier, Castel ⓣ 01481 256 531 ⓛ Open daily for lunch and evening meals; bar food not available Sun evenings

ⓞ *Fort Grey on Rocquaine Bay houses a fascinating museum*

St Peter in the Wood & Torteval
cliffs and surf

Southwestern Guernsey and the parishes of St Peter in the Wood (known locally as St Pierre du Bois) and Torteval have a strikingly varied shoreline. The west coast, scalloped into wide, low-lying bays of rock and sand, changes dramatically between high and low tide when the reefs lie exposed. With mighty Atlantic breakers, the coastline is popular with expert surfers, but novice swimmers should take care.

Round the dramatic Pleinmont headland on the southwestern tip, the coast takes on a completely different character. Here the shoreline is cliff-fringed and rocky, hiding tiny, tidal scraps of sand. The waterline can be difficult and dangerous to reach along clifftop footpaths: take a picnic and enjoy the breezy scenery and wild flowers.

Defensive structures line this daunting coast, from Martello towers to German gun emplacements. Most impressive is the gaunt tower in

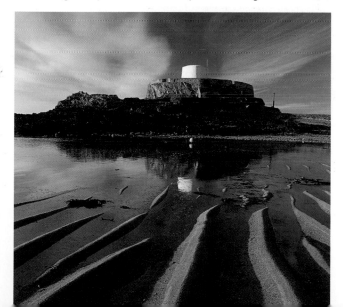

Pleinmont. Inland are the parishes of Torteval, St Peter in the Wood and St Saviour (see page 30), which are less developed than other parts of the island. Quiet farmland is interspersed with a web of tiny rural lanes where you can get thoroughly and enjoyably lost.

Be sure to drive carefully along the west coast road in rough weather when the tide is in. Alarmingly, the waves sometimes wash right over the sea walls. However, in fine weather, the western seafront can be magical, especially at sunset when the rocks turn extraordinary hues of pink and gold. Watch it from the fortified headlands, where parking places can be reached by quiet access tracks off the comparatively busy main road.

THINGS TO SEE & DO

Cliff walks ★★★
Guernsey's hilly south coast is the prettiest part of the island for walking. Footpaths lead all the way along the coast, past watchtowers, coves and headlands – it is free of traffic but accessible by lanes with parking places at various points. Cliffs may be unstable; don't stray from the marked paths.

Coach House Gallery ★★
Housed in sympathetically restored farm buildings, this light, airy gallery displays works by local artists, including crafts and original prints at a wide range of prices. Visit the Framecraft art shop across the courtyard for artists' materials or a speedy framing service. ⓐ Les Paysans Road, St Peter in the Wood ⓣ 01481 265 339 ⓛ Open 11.00–17.00 all year ⓘ Admission free

Fort Grey ★★
The stumpy white Martello tower on Rocquaine Bay contains a fascinating Shipwreck Museum, showing the perils of Guernsey's reef-strewn west coast. ⓐ Rocquaine Coast Road, St Peter in the Wood ⓣ 01481 265 036 ⓛ Open 10.00–17.00 (April–Oct) ⓘ Admission charge

Lihou Island ★

The tiny, privately owned island of Lihou, off the L'Erée headland, makes an unusual walk at low tide. There is just one house and the remains of a Benedictine priory. Check tide tables carefully before you cross; the causeway is uncovered only for a few hours.

RESTAURANTS & PUBS

This part of the island has a good range of eating places, including some of Guernsey's best. Most are easy to find along the larger roads, but you'll need a good navigator for the **Café du Moulin**.

Café du Moulin ££ Rapidly establishing a name as one of Guernsey's foremost restaurants, this delightful old mill huddles in one of the island's greenest valleys. Teas and bar snacks are offered, as well as imaginative, full menus. Everything is freshly prepared, and there are vegetarian choices. ❸ Rue de Quanteraine, St Peter in the Wood ❶ 01481 265 944 ● Open daily (except Mon and Sun evenings) ❶ Book ahead; no smoking in the dining room

Imperial Hotel ££ Three bars, plus a patio and garden, offer a choice of places to enjoy some excellent cooking near a lovely stretch of coastline with cliff walks and beaches. ❸ Pleinmont, Torteval ❶ 01481 264 044 ● Open daily; huge carvery on Sun

Longfrie Inn £ This family-oriented country inn has plenty of satisfying but inexpensive bar food, along with cheerful menus for children, a garden and a play area. ❸ Rue de Longfrie, St Peter in the Wood ❶ 01481 263 107 ● Open for lunch and evening meals (except Mon and Sun evenings)

Taste of India ££ This traditional-looking cottage, known as Sunset Cottage, offers an exotic Indian-inspired menu. No extra charge for technicolour sunsets or a stroll along the strand. ❸ L'Erée, St Peter in the Wood ❶ 01481 264 516 ● Open daily from noon

Forest, St Martin & St Andrew
sheltered coves and countryside

The main roads close to St Peter Port are built up and congested with a surprising amount of rush-hour commuter traffic, but brief detours down the quiet lanes of St Martin lead to the idyllic, unspoilt headlands of Icart and Jerbourg, where quiet sandy coves nestle beneath dramatic cliffs. Icart is the highest headland on Guernsey.

More sheltered than the west coast or northern beaches, these coves are ideal for swimming, though some involve a steep trek. The best way to see this part of the island is on foot; follow the waymarked coastal tracks that follow the coast or direct you inland to the St Andrew countryside. Alternatively, take a boat trip from St Peter Port harbour on a fine day and view the south coast from the sea.

THINGS TO SEE & DO
Catherine Best Studio★

One of Guernsey's most renowned jewellery designers has a studio showroom in a converted windmill. Original, handmade pieces using precious and semi-precious materials, in a wide range of traditional and modern designs. The Old Mill, Steam Mill Lanes, St Martin 01481 237 771 Open Mon–Sat 09.00–17.30, Sun 09.30–17.00 Admission free

German Occupation Museum ★★

An authentic display of World War II memorabilia is on display here, recounting Occupation days in Guernsey. The day-to-day trials of the islanders are brought vividly to life in crystal sets, diaries, press cuttings and ration books. Tea rooms (try some wartime parsnip coffee – if you dare). Located near Forest parish church (opposite the airport entrance turning) 01481 238 205 Open Tues–Sun 10.00–17.00; winter times vary Admission charge

🔺 Visit the tunnels of the German Underground Hospital in St Andrew

○ *Shells decorate the Little Chapel, near Guernsey Clockmakers*

German Underground Hospital ★★

This dank, rambling tunnel complex, dug by slave labour, is one of the most chilling reminders of the German Occupation period on any of the Channel Islands. Despite the effort expended in its construction, it was scarcely used for medical purposes, and served mainly as an ammunition dump. ⓐ La Vassalerie Road, St Andrew ① 01481 239 100 ⓛ Open 10.00–noon and 14.00–16.00 (June); until 16.30 (July– Aug); restricted hours in winter ① Admission charge

Guernsey Clockmakers & Little Chapel ★★

An amazing collection of barometers and timepieces, from longcase clocks to novelty watches, many made on the premises. Nearby stands the photogenic Little Chapel, claimed to be the world's smallest church at only 5 m (16 ft) long. Inspired by the grotto shrine at Lourdes, it is smothered with shells, pebbles and fragments of coloured china. ⓐ Les Vauxbelets, St Andrew ① 01481 236 360 ⓛ Clockmakers open Mon–Fri 08.30–17.30 and Sat 10.00–16.00 ① Admission free; chapel freely accessible all year; donations welcome

La Gran'mère du Chimquière ★

This ancient Bronze Age curiosity, whose name means 'the graveyard granny', stands by the gate of St Martin's parish church. A female figure carved in stone, she is believed to have magical powers and, even today, flower garlands and good-luck tokens are placed on her head, especially after wedding ceremonies. ⓐ St Martin's Church ① Admission free

⬥ Gran'mère du Chimquière

Moulin Huet Pottery ★

A cottage workshop gallery hidden in a leafy lane leading to a pretty south-coast cove. The painter Renoir was inspired by this part of the island on a visit in 1882. Porcelain, stoneware, paintings and crafts on sale, or you can simply watch the pottery being made. ⓐ Moulin Huet, St Martin ⓣ 01481 237 201 ⓛ Open Mon–Sat 09.00–16.00, Sun 10.00–noon (Easter to Christmas only) ⓘ Admission free

Sausmarez Manor ★★★

This impressive stately home is occupied by one of the oldest and most distinguished families in the Channel Islands. Entertaining guided tours of the house highlight fine furnishings and ancestral anecdotes. Additional attractions include exotic woodland gardens, a miniature railway and a challenging pitch-and-putt course, plus a new sculpture trail. ⓐ Sausmarez Road, St Martin ⓣ 01481 235 571 ⓛ Open Mon–Thurs 10.30 and 11.30 (Easter–Oct), plus afternoons (June–Sept); other attractions open 10.00–17.00 ⓘ Separate admission charges

RESTAURANTS

Many of the most appealing restaurants in this part of the island are in beautifully located hotels. Full meals can be a bit pricey, but most places offer less formal bar snacks or teas too.

Bella Luce ££ This long-established manor hotel in a rural setting is an island favourite. Bar meals and afternoon teas are served in the gardens on fine days, with traditional à la carte fare in the evenings. ⓐ La Fosse, St Martin ⓣ 01481 238 764 ⓛ Open daily

Le Chalet ££ Nestling in woodland above Fermain Bay, this alpine-style restaurant offers a sun terrace and bar for light refreshments, as well as its more lavish French restaurant. ⓐ Fermain Bay, St Martin ⓣ 01481 235 716 ⓛ Open for lunch and evening meals (April–Oct)

FOREST, ST MARTIN & ST ANDREW

Idlerocks Hotel ££ Following a devastating fire the hotel stopped serving meals but its team plans to reopen the restaurant soon. A superb seaview setting in one of Guernsey's quietest spots makes a meal here special so it is worth checking to see if it has reopened in time for your visit. ➌ Jerbourg Point, St Martin ☎ 01481 237 711

▲ *Pleasant pursuits at Sausmarez Manor*

41

Herm
jewel in the sand

Tiny Herm – a mere 20-minute ferry-hop from Guernsey's St Peter Port – makes a marvellous outing for a fine day. With no cars or organised attractions, Herm Island offers a deceptively simple but captivating mix of beautiful scenery, idyllic beaches and an irresistible invitation to relax and unwind.

Just 2.5 km (1½ miles) long and 1 km (½ mile) wide, you can walk round Herm in under two hours. Near the harbour stands a spotless Mediterranean-style 'village' colourwashed in ice-cream pastels and consisting of a hotel, pubs and a handful of little shops. Here you can have a drink, a snack or an excellent meal, and investigate an imaginative range of souvenirs on sale at good prices.

Central paths take you through woods and fields past the Tenant's castellated Manor and a tiny medieval chapel. Some outbuildings are converted into self-catering cottages, and the Seagull camp-ground nestles discreetly among the trees. A pedigree herd of placid Guernsey cattle grazes in the surrounding farmland.

If you strike south, you climb along cliff paths overlooking rocks and

◭ *Belvoir Bay, with Shell Beach beyond*

reefs, and the privately-owned neighbouring island of **Jethou** (not accessible to visitors). The low-lying northern routes lead over heathland fringed by glorious belts of sand. Everywhere on Herm, wildlife flourishes in hosts of seabirds, clouds of butterflies and riotous flowers, while farm gates, fences, beach cafés and holiday cottages are kept in top order.

> The early morning 'milk boat' ferry offers a reduced day return to Herm – and a longer stay on the island. Remember to listen to the weather forecast as you'll be out of doors for much of the time.

THINGS TO SEE & DO
La Pierre aux Rats ★
A large prehistoric standing stone served as a seamark for centuries until quarrymen removed it in the 19th century, thinking it was just another useful lump of granite. Local sailors protested strenuously, and the present obelisk was put in its place.

Le Manoir ★
Herm's real 'village' centres round the imposing 15th-century manor, now the residence of the Wood family. The medieval-looking 'keep' is only a century old. Near the manor house are the island's power station, workshops and unobtrusive modern farm buildings.

Neolithic dolmens ★
In ancient times, Herm was considered a sacred place and served as a burial ground. Traces of several stone tombs remain towards the north of the island.

St Tugual's Chapel ★★
This quaint little building dates from the 11th century, and its unusual belltower remains its most striking feature. The chapel also contains attractive stained glass, and a memorial to the Tenant's wife. Informal services are held every Sunday.

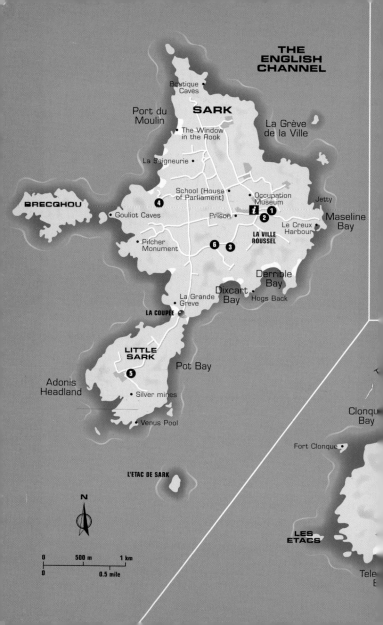

THE
ENGLISH
CHANNEL

SARK

Boutique
Caves

Port du
Moulin

La Grève
de la Ville

The Window
in the Rook

La Seigneurie •

School (House
of Parliament)

Occupation
Museum

Jetty

BRECQHOU

④

• Gouliot Caves

Prison •

ℹ ①

②

Le Creux
Harbour

Maseline
Bay

**LA VILLE
ROUSSEL**

• Pilcher
Monument

⑥ ③

Derrible
Bay

Dixcart
Bay

La Grande
Grève

Hogs Back

LA COUPÉE

**LITTLE
SARK**

⑤

Pot Bay

Clonqu
Bay

Adonis
Headland

• Silver mines

Fort Clonque •

• Venus Pool

L'ETAC DE SARK

N

**LES
ETACS**

| 0 | 500 m | 1 km |

| 0 | 0.5 mile |

Tele
E

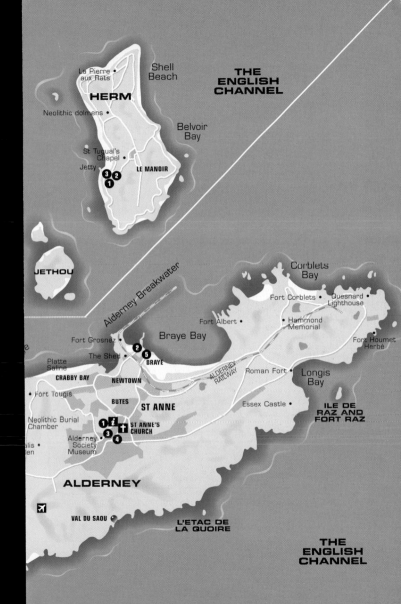

THE
ENGLISH
CHANNEL

La Pierre
aux Rats •

Shell
Beach

HERM

Neolithic dolmens •

Belvoir
Bay

St Tugual's
Chapel

Jetty •

❸❷
❶

LE MANOIR

JETHOU

Corblets
Bay

Alderney Breakwater

Fort Corblets •

Quesnard •
Lighthouse

Fort Albert •

Fort Grosnez •

Braye Bay

Hammond
Memorial

Fort Houmet
Herbé

The Shed •

❷❺
BRAYE

Platte
Saline

ALDERNEY
RAILWAY

Roman Fort •

Longis
Bay

CRABBY BAY

NEWTOWN

• Fort Tougis

BUTES

ST ANNE

Essex Castle •

ILE DE
RAZ AND
FORT RAZ

Neolithic Burial
Chamber

❶ℹ
❸❶
❹
ST ANNE'S
CHURCH

...alis
...en

Alderney •
Society
Museum

ALDERNEY

✈

VAL DU SAOU •

L'ETAC DE
LA QUOIRE

THE
ENGLISH
CHANNEL

Herm has a few 'house rules' designed to maintain its peaceful attractions. Visitors are requested to keep pets under control, and not to pick plants, leave litter or play transistor radios in public.

BEACHES

Herm's pride and joy is **Shell Beach**, on the northeastern shore. This magnificent stretch of sparkling quartz and shell fragments looks truly tropical on a fine day and is the perfect place for beachcombing, sunbathing and sandcastles. Rock pools trap fascinating pockets of sealife at low tide, and the clear, gently shelving water is ideal for snorkelling. As the name suggests, the sand consists of millions of sparkling shells, whole or fragmented, some carried from the tropics on the Gulf Stream.

Herm's northern coast is an almost continuous belt of sand and dunes at low tide, easily reached if you're prepared to walk. Near the harbour the shoreline is muddier and rockier, good for messing about with a shrimping net. **Belvoir Bay** is a more intimate sandy cove further south (beware strong currents at low tide) with a café and toilets.

RESTAURANTS (see map on pages 44–45)

Some summer ferry deals include lunch or dinner with your boat fare, but Herm operates seasonally, and in the winter the island's pubs and cafés may be closed. Check facilities before you sail. There are no grocery shops, but you can always take a picnic. Herm oysters are famed throughout the Channel Islands.

🔺 *Herm is a 20-minute ferry hop from Guernsey*

46

HERM'S TENANT

In 1949, Major Peter Wood and his wife took over a long lease on the island from the Crown. Their hard work and enthusiastic enterprise has resulted in today's civilised miniature paradise. Financed by dairy farming and tourism, Herm is still managed by members of the Wood family. The population of 50 is doubled in summer by seasonal staff. Local children are educated in the tiny island school. Herm generates its own electricity and has its own water and drainage systems. Morning boats transport about 200 gallons of creamy milk daily to Guernsey for processing, and offload the empty churns with Herm-bound passengers in the afternoon.

The Mermaid Tavern £ ❶ The 'village inn', with good snacks, and full lunchtime and evening meals most of the year. Summer barbecues with tables outside, and roaring fires in chilly weather.
☎ 01481 710 170 🕑 Open daily (summer); Tues, Wed, Fri and Sat (winter)

The Ship Inn ££ ❷ This pleasant pub-restaurant is part of the White House hotel (see below), offering lunchtime fare and more elaborate evening meals at the Captain's Table (inclusive ferry/dinner packages available). ☎ 01481 722 159 🕑 Open daily (April–Oct)

The White House £££ ❸ Herm's only hotel caters primarily for resident guests but, space permitting, day visitors may book ahead for a table, for dinner only. ☎ 01481 722 159 🕑 Open daily (April–Oct) ❶ Smart dress requested; no smoking in the dining room

NIGHTLIFE

If sea air, good food and exercise don't suggest an early night, you may find yourself practising the age-old but much-neglected art of conversation. To encourage social interaction, television is deliberately banished at Herm's White House Hotel.

Sark
feudal showcase

Situated 9.5 km (6 miles) east of Guernsey is the quaint political
fossil of Sark – a last vestige of European feudalism. Its unique status
comes from being the smallest independent 'state' in the British
Commonwealth. Less than 5 sq km (2 sq miles), Sark supports about 550
permanent residents and welcomes over a hundred times as many visitors every year. Five hours or so between ferry rides is short shrift to give
this pretty place. Stay longer if you can – especially in spring, when the
island is carpeted with flowers.

◆ *Beneath La Coupée lies Grand Grève Bay*

Sark is a jagged rock plateau perching on 90 m (300 ft) high cliffs, gashed by deep valleys leading to the sea. It is almost two islands, for the smaller southerly island, called Little Sark, is only attached to its big sister by a knife-edge ridge called **La Coupée**. Sark's scenery and individuality attract enough daytrippers to cause bicycle jams in high season. But if you stray off the beaten tracks, you will find secret coves and crevices all to yourself.

Like its close neighbour, Herm, Sark allows no visiting motor vehicles, and access to the island is by ferry only (helicopters or light aircraft may land in dire emergencies only). A tractor-bus service saves ferry passengers the half-mile climb up and down **Harbour Hill**. At the top of the hill lies a village of Toytown proportions.

The island's famous Dame Sibil Hathaway, remembered for her courage during the German occupation, has been succeeded as Seigneur of Sark by her grandson, whose residence, **La Seigneurie**, is Sark's most impressive building. The Seigneur still holds a few privileges first granted by Elizabeth I in 1565. He is the only Sark-dweller permitted to keep doves, for example, or an unspayed bitch. More lucratively, he is entitled to receive one-thirteenth (Le Trezième) of the value of any Sark property that changes hands.

No boats run on Sundays on Sark, when some of the island services close down. If you're based on this island for a while, this can be a delightfully uncrowded time to explore. Even better – at night, there are no street lights to mask the stars.

THINGS TO SEE & DO
Boat trips ★
If you're only on Sark for a day, a boat-trip is a bit ambitious, but in calm weather it's an enjoyable way to see Sark's intricate, cave-pocked cliffs, study the wide variety of seabirds and take in the salty air. **Sark Tourist Information Centre** has more detailed information on how to arrange a trip. ⓐ Harbour Hill ☎ 01481 832 345

Carriage rides ★

See Sark the leisurely way – by horsepower. Patient carthorses await the ferry boats in summer. You can pre-book a jaunt from Guernsey, or negotiate the fare on arrival for one or two-hour excursions.
❶ 01481 832 345

La Coupée ★★

This breathtaking neck of rock, linking Little Sark to the main island, was fenced by prisoners-of-war, and is just wide enough for a tractor or a horse-drawn carriage to pass across, with dizzying drops to either side.

La Seigneurie ★★

You can't look round the Seigneur's granite manor house, but his varied, beautiful gardens are well worth seeing, with their roses, tender plants, a hedge maze and a Victorian greenhouse. Look out for the strange Gothic colombier (dovecote) and the antique cannon. **❶** 01481 832 345 **🕐** Open Mon–Fri 10.00–17.00 (Easter–Oct), plus Sat and Sun (high summer) **❶** Admission charge

Le Creux Harbour ★

Tunnels lead to this pretty, rock-walled harbour from the more modern and practical landing stage at La Maseline.

Prison ★

Sark's curious little jail stands in the village. It has just two cells, and is still occasionally used to detain miscreants before dispatching them to Guernsey for trial.

Occupation Museum ★★

This museum highlights aspects of island life under the jackboot during World War II, including photographs of the redoubtable Dame of Sark dealing with her uninvited guests. Sark escaped fairly lightly, with no serious food shortages and no fortifications. **❶** 01481 832 345 **🕐** Open Easter–Sept **❶** Admission charge

Silver mines ★
The shafts and ventilation chimneys of Sark's 19th-century mining days can still be seen on Little Sark. The mines were never profitable, and were abandoned after a tragedy in 1845.

BEACHES
Access to most of Sark's cliff-backed coves involves a steep climb. Easiest to reach (from Dixcart Hotel) is **Dixcart Bay** – safe, sandy and scenic, spanned by an arch of natural rock. Neighbouring **Derrible Bay** has sand only at low tide. Adventurous explorers may discover **Pot Bay** or the deep tidal **Venus Pool** on Little Sark.

RESTAURANTS (see map on pages 44–45)
Sark's most sophisticated eating places are its hotel-restaurants, several of which vie for placings in good food guides. If all you want is a drink or a snack, no problem. Choice is restricted in winter when most hotels close. Buy picnic provisions and cakes at the village's Island Stores.

◗ *The traditional way of getting around Sark*

Aval du Creux Hotel ££ **1** Simple lunches, cream teas, and dinner in a pleasant setting, with tables outside. **a** Next to tourist office on Harbour Hill **t** 01481 832 036 **l** Open 11.00–17.30 (April–Oct)

Bel Air Inn £ **2** This inn has a contemporary feel, and offers a good choice of dishes with the emphasis on seafood, steaks and pasta. **a** Harbour Hill **t** 01481 832 053 **l** Open daily

Dixcart Bay Hotel ££ **3** One of Sark's oldest and most respected hotels (pronounced 'dee-cart') welcomes non-residents with a tasty range of snacks and meals, including children's menus and seafood specials. **a** Dixcart Valley **t** 01481 832 015 **l** Open all year

Hotel Petit Champ ££ **4** A west-coast setting with sea views accompanies everything from sandwiches to candlelit dinners here. There is a sheltered garden, and lobster and crab are available. **a** On the West coast; from the Methodist Chapel follow hotel signs towards sea **t** 01481 832 046 **l** Open Easter–Oct

La Sablonnerie Hotel ££ **5** A charming garden setting is just one of the attractions of this acclaimed farmhouse hotel. Fresh fish and home-grown produce, Sark cream teas and seafood platters are also featured. **a** Little Sark **t** 01481 832 061 **l** Open Easter–Oct

Stocks Island Hotel ££ **6** The Courtyard Bistro in this hotel offers a good range of snacks, teas, light and full meals, with more elaborate dining in the hotel's Cider Press Restaurant. Regular Chinese and Indian evenings, as well as children's menus and tables outside. **a** Dixcart Valley **t** 01481 832 001 **l** Open 10.00–22.00 (April–Oct)

NIGHTLIFE

Sark's social scene revolves around the Island Hall in the village centre, which has table tennis, badminton and a billiard table. Just occasionally in summer, concerts and recitals are held.

⬤ *Brecqhou – a very private island*

AN ISLAND OF YOUR OWN

'So, you like my island, Mr Bond ...' A separate island, **Brecqhou**, lies a stone's throw off Sark's northern tip. This was privately purchased in 1993 by the wealthy Barclay brothers – twin businessmen whose reclusive entrepreneurial activities cause much local gossip. Passing ferries give a tantalising glimpse of a huge newly built Gothic castle rising from Brecqhou. This extraordinary lair was constructed by a Guernsey workforce sworn to secrecy. Rumours of nuclear bunkers, summit conferences and private casinos flourish, fuelled by vigorous denials, and determined resistance to trespassing.

Alderney
windswept delight

Alderney, the most northerly of the Channel Islands, lies just 13 km (8 miles) west of Normandy's Cotentin peninsula. The island is just 2.5 km (1½ miles) wide and 5.5 km (3½ miles) long and is the perfect place to unwind, offering something for almost everyone.

It does not take long to get to Alderney from Guernsey, or indeed to discover the attractions of its unspoilt open landscapes, wonderful cliff walks and beautiful uncrowded beaches. Good leisure facilities and

friendly pubs and restaurants add to the island's natural charms. At its heart lies the delightful town of **St Anne**, while Victorian fortresses stud the headlands.

The island is home to numerous species of wildlife, flowers and marine life. There are two renowned nature reserves operated by the Wildlife Trust. **Longis Nature Reserve** is divided into 13 different habitats from intertidal and coastal Heathland to freshwater ponds, grasslands and woodland. Alderney's second reserve, **Val du Saou**, focuses on the island's only coastal woodland valley, where trees and bird life thrive. It is also home to the leucistic (blonde) hedgehog.

Alderney was the first Channel Island to introduce duty-free goods. Alcohol and tobacco prices are certainly worth checking wherever you see the sign, but do your research first on other items. You may buy only if you are leaving the Bailiwick of Guernsey directly after your stay (eg heading for Jersey or the UK).

BREAKWATERS

Alderney's huge breakwater has another interesting story. Built as part of the UK's defence strategy, and now essential to Alderney's economy (no seaborne freight could be landed without it), it has inevitably suffered periodic storm damage and its maintenance costs are phenomenal. After the Falklands War, Guernsey agreed to pick up the tab for Alderney's breakwater as its contribution to the British defence budget.

THINGS TO SEE & DO
Alderney Breakwater ★★
This huge Victorian granite structure, maintained by Guernsey, extends over half a mile into the sea.

◀ *Sheltered Braye Bay is ideal for swimming and windsurfing*

Alderney Society Museum ★★

Housed in an old school, this small collection traces the island's history from prehistoric times. ⓐ Lower High Street, St Anne ☏ 01481 823 222 🕒 Open Mon–Fri 10.00–noon and 14.00–16.00, Sat and Sun 10.00–noon (April–Oct) ❶ Admission charge

Alderney Railway ★★

The Channel Islands' last remaining railway, built to carry granite to the breakwater, offers 30-minute nostalgia rides in old London Underground carriages in summer. Adults and children can also enjoy a ride in summer on the miniature railway in Mannez Quarry. ☏ 01481 822 980 🕒 Open weekends and Bank Holidays 14.00–16.45 (summer) ❶ Admission charge

Boat trips ★★

Trips on Voyager or Lady Maris survey Alderney's coastal scenery or hop to France and the other Channel Islands. Seasonal and weather-dependent. The **Alderney Tourist Information Centre** (ⓐ Victoria Street ☏ 01481 823 737) has detailed information on trips.

Fort Clonque ★

One of Alderney's Victorian forts, attractively restored by the Landmark Trust as holiday apartments, lies at the end of a concrete causeway and is inaccessible at high tide (no admission to inside of fort).

Hammond Memorial ★

Plaques in several languages commemorate the Russian, Polish and Jewish slave-workers who perished under German occupation while constructing Hitler's Atlantic Wall.

Les Etacs Rocks ★★

Alderney is home to one of the British Isles' rare gannet colonies, and here, the birds sit beak to beak in a pungent top-dressing of guano.

In a spectacular setting, Fort Clonque is cut off from the mainland at high tide

Nearby Burhou Island is home to a small group of puffins. Don't forget your binoculars if you're a keen birdwatcher

Quesnard Lighthouse ★
Dating from 1912, the Quesnard Lighthouse offers spectacular views of the razor-sharp reefs on this dangerous coast. Afternoon visits by arrangement with the tourist office. ❶ 01481 823 737

St Anne's Church ★★
One of the finest Channel Island churches, built of Caen stone and restored after wartime damage.

⬤ *The restored interior of St Anne's Church (see page 57)*

Telegraph Tower ★
The high cliffs near this 19th-century signalling tower offer views of all the Channel Islands.

The Shed ★★
Items from a wrecked Elizabethan warship are displayed in this museum. ⓐ Braye Harbour ① 01481 823 222 ⓛ Open some afternoons in summer; check with Alderney Society Museum (see page 56) ① Admission free

BEACHES

Alderney has some good stretches of sand on its northern shores, mostly fairly easy to reach. Some of the fastest tidal races in the world flow past the island. Cliffs make the southerly shore difficult to reach. The varied seabirds make Alderney's coastal walks interesting, but the many fortresses, some derelict, give it a forbidding air. Best for swimming and windsurfing is **Braye Bay**, protected from westerly gales by the breakwater. Quieter **Corblets Bay** is dominated by Fort Corblets and has safe bathing and good surf. **Longis Bay** – another sheltered stretch of sand on the eastern coast – is also popular.

RESTAURANTS (see map on pages 44–45)

Alderney offers good eating and drinking places, nearly all of them clustered in St Anne or Braye Bay. Prices are slightly higher than the other islands due to freight costs, but licensing hours are more lenient; pubs stay open all day and every day, including Sunday. Seafood lovers should not miss the Seafood Festival in May.

Bumps Eating House ££ ❶ Charming atmosphere with an impressive menu featuring international cuisine and an extensive wine list. ⓐ Braye Street, St Anne ❶ 01481 823 197

First and Last ££ ❷ Primarily a seafood restaurant serving mouth-watering food that appeals to the eye and the taste buds. ⓐ Braye Harbour ❶ 01481 823 162

Gannets £ ❸ Attractive day-time café, licensed bistro and evening wine-bar in a light, airy dining room decorated with soothing seascapes. There is friendly service, and summer tables outside. ⓐ Victoria Street, St Anne ❶ 01481 823 098

Georgian House ££ ❹ Civilised hotel-restaurant in elegant period building. Specialities include seafood, barbecues and

traditional Sunday roasts. Good-value lunchtime bar menus, but
more expensive restaurant food only in evenings. ⓐ Victoria Street,
St Anne ❶ 01481 822 471 ⓛ Open daily for lunch; Wed–Mon for evening
meals ⓘ Best to book

The Moorings £ ⑤ Traditional, good-value bar meals, a la carte
menu with great seafood and al fresco dining around the BBQ
in summer. ⓐ Braye Harbour ❶ 01481 822 421 ⓛ Open daily

NIGHTLIFE

Only the larger islands offer anything significant in the way of nightlife,
and evening entertainment on Alderney is more likely to involve a jigsaw
puzzle, a game of Scrabble or a good book than a night on the tiles. Most
hotels provide books and board games for evenings and wet days, and
impromptu events, such as quiz nights or live music, may take place in
local pubs occasionally. Alderney's evening entertainment mostly centres
on pubs and restaurants. Visitors are welcome to join in local island
happenings – talks, slide shows, whist drives, etc. You can generally
find a game of whist, dominoes or bridge, or a darts match, going
on somewhere, and there's a tiny cinema in Victoria Street.

EXCURSIONS
Out & about

Bailiwick beach tour
sand and pebble attractions

Depending how you count them, the Bailiwick's islands have something like 27 separate beaches. They vary from grand scalloped bays, on Guernsey's low-lying western and northern coasts, to sheltered coves in deep green hills. Take your pick, but check the wind direction first. Huge tides make a great difference to the appearance of local beaches. If you swim or venture into rock formations or across causeways, always check the tide tables. The first run-down reads clockwise from St Peter Port on Guernsey, with separate lists for Herm, Sark and Alderney.

Havelet Bay This popular town beach is where Victor Hugo took his daily dips when he lived in St Peter Port. A scenic setting of wooded cliffs and views of Castle Cornet add to its attractions. Covered at high tide. Seawater tidal pools at La Valette. Easy access (car or bus), cafés, toilets.

Soldier's Bay This is a rocky bay with no facilities. There is access via a cliff path, and views to Herm.

Fermain Bay This beautiful, sheltered cove is often pictured in brochures, showing its sand backed by pebbles at low tide. There is access by boat, bus or cliff path, and it has very clean water, a café and toilets. Parking is virtually non-existent.

Petit Port Gorgeous, south-facing sandy cove, which is kept reasonably quiet by its challenging 270 access steps, but remains popular with locals. There are no facilities.

Moulin Huet This beach captivated Renoir in the 1880s and has a lovely setting that includes caves. Parking is nearby, but some walking is necessary. See the **Moulin Huet Pottery** while you're here, which also has a good teashop.

Saints Bay A peaceful bay, with snorkelling, but no parking.

Petit Bot A large, picturesque cove, sheltered by a headland. There is access by bus or from a nearby car park – follow the stream down the lane. There is a café here. Beware of the adjacent cove (Le Portelet) – the exit is cut off at high tide. Several other difficult-to-reach coves can be glimpsed beneath the Icart peninsula.

🔺 *Almost tropical, the beautiful Fermain Bay*

South coast Between Petit Bot and Pleinmont Point there is no accessible sand, just a lovely stretch of cliffs hugged by a footpath. The scenery becomes steadily wilder towards the west, culminating in an Atlantic promontory guarded by fortresses. Out to sea is the Hanois Lighthouse.

Portelet Bay This exposed, west-facing beach is a mix of rocks and sand, with a small harbour. Easy to reach by car or bus, with toilets, parking and refreshments. There is a good bar at the nearby Imperial Hotel.

Rocquaine Bay An extension of the wide sand-and-rock Portelet Bay, but separated from Portelet by Fort Grey, now housing the Shipwreck Museum. There is a crafts centre and café opposite. At the north end are Fort Saumarez and Lihou Island (low tide access only).

L'Erée This bay reveals a wide crescent of pale sand at high tide, and has good facilities and safe bathing. There is a pleasant Indian restaurant opposite, a craft shop and a café.

Perelle Bay Mostly rock here, but with pleasant headlands to either side. Visit **Le Tricoteur knitwear factory** while you're here.

Vazon Bay This bay features a huge scoop of sand divided by reefs. Surfing and sand-racing take place here, and the gently shelving beach is safe for paddling in calm weather. Good sunsets and plenty of facilities. Visit Fort Hommet at the northern end.

Cobo/Saline Bay This bay consists of a sand belt broken up by reefs – it is scenic at low water and backed by dunes to the north. There are plenty of facilities; public transport, fish and chips, shops and hotels. At high tide, the sea often washes over the seawall.

Port Soif A cosy, horseshoe-shaped bay with large rocks backed by dunes and rock pools at low tide. Sheltered sand, but dangerous low-tide currents at the mouth of the bay.

Portinfer A beach with soft white sand, dunes and rock pools.

Le Grand Havre/Ladies Bay A large, complex bay with white sand, rocks and dunes, and a small harbour. See the Rousse Tower while you're here. Easier to reach with a car; the buses follow the main road.

Pembroke/L'Ancresse Bay Very large, sheltered beach, with safe wind-surfing and cafés. Quiet common and golf course behind.

Bordeaux Harbour/Petils Bay Quiet, low-lying beaches with a fishing harbour and views of Herm, but some dangerous low tide currents. Beaucette Marina, with its stylish ocean-going yachts, is tucked into an old quarry in the northeastern tip. Vale Castel guards it to the south.

HERM
Shell Beach This beach is Herm's pride and joy. A magnificent stretch of sparkling quartz and shell fragments looks truly tropical on a fine day and is the perfect place for beachcombing, sunbathing and sandcastles.

Belvoir Bay An intimate sandy cove, Belvoir Bay is good for relaxation, but take care as it is renowned for its strong currents at low tide.

SARK
Dixcart Bay A safe, sandy and scenic bay, spanned by an arch of natural rock. A relaxing and fun visit.

Derrible Bay A pretty bay that has sand only at low tide.

Pot Bay This bay is difficult to reach because of the rock formation and only really accessible to adventurous explorers.

Venus Pool Situated on Little Sark, this bay has very deep water and is tidal, but very dramatic.

ALDERNEY
Braye Bay Protected from westerly gales, this is ideal for swimmers.

Corblets Bay The quiet bay is dominated by Fort Corblets and has safe bathing and good surf.

Longis Bay A sheltered stretch of sand on the eastern coast, popular with swimmers and families.

Wherever you stay, Guernsey island is small enough to allow you to choose your beach by wind direction and sun position. The beaches of south-eastern Guernsey are a good bet when westerly or northerly winds are blowing, and they tend to be sunniest in the early part of the day.

GROSNEZ

Plèmont Bay

Sorel

PLÉMONT

PORTINFER

Grève de Lecq

Devil's Hole

North Coast Visitor Centre

La Mare Vineyards

ST JOHN'S CHUR

MILAIS

B35

B55

B65

B40

C103

B33

LEOVILLE

L'ETACQ

Battle of Flowers Museum

Bouchet Agateware Pottery

Catherina Best Studio

ST MARY'S PARISH CHURCH

Jersey (

Jersey Pearl

ST OUEN

ST MARY

Hampton Country I Muse

Le Moulin de Quétivel Kempt Tower

ST OUEN'S CHURCH

St Ouen's Manor

A12

ST LAWRE

Living Legend

ST LAWRENCE'S CHURCH

i

ST PETER'S PARISH CHURCH

Jersey Motor Museum

A11

St Ouen's Bay

B35

Le Moulin de Quétivel

Jersey Tunnel Under Hospit

ST PETER

BEL ROYAL

A12

ST BRELADE

Quennevais Sports Centre

BEAUMONT

A1

La Moye Golf Course

ST BRELADES Fisherman's Chapel

Jersey Lavender Farm

A13

Shell Garden

ST AUBIN

St A E

LA PULENTE

Petit Port

LA CORBIÈRE

Corbière Lighthouse

LA MOYE

St Brelade's Bay

Ouaisné Bay

Beauport

Portelet Bay

N

0   2 km

0   1 mile

THE ENGLISH CHANNEL

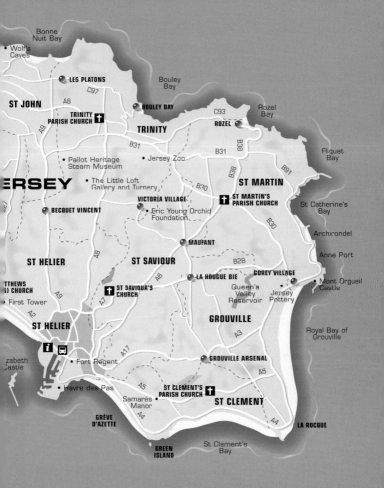

THE ENGLISH CHANNEL

Bonne
Nuit Bay
• Wolf's
Caves

• LES PLATONS

C97

Bouley
Bay

ST JOHN

A8

• BOULEY BAY

Rozel
Bay

TRINITY
PARISH CHURCH ✝

C93

TRINITY

ROZEL

Fliquet
Bay

B31

B38

B31

• Jersey Zoo

B38

B91

• Pallot Heritage
Steam Museum

ERSEY

• The Little Loft
Gallery and Turnery

B30

ST MARTIN

VICTORIA VILLAGE

✝ ST MARTIN'S
PARISH CHURCH

St Catherine's
Bay

• BECQUET VINCENT

• Eric Young Orchid
Foundation

B30

Archirondel

• MAUFANT

Anne Port

ST HELIER

A8

ST SAVIOUR

B2B

TTHEWS
S) CHURCH

A8

✝ ST SAVIOUR'S
CHURCH

A7

• LA HOGUE BIE

GOREY VILLAGE

• Mont Orgueil
Castle

• First Tower

A9

Queen's
Valley
Reservoir

Jersey
Pottery

A2

ST HELIER

GROUVILLE

Royal Bay of
Grouville

A17

ℹ 🚌

zabeth
Castle

• Fort Regent

A5

• GROUVILLE ARSENAL

A5

• Havre des Pas

A5

ST CLEMENT'S
PARISH CHURCH ✝

ST CLEMENT

A4

GRÈVE
D'AZETTE

Samarès
Manor

A4

LA ROCQUE

GREEN
ISLAND

St Clement's
Bay

St Helier, Jersey
seat of parliament

Jersey is only an hour away from St Peter Port, Guernsey, by ferry and is well worth a visit. The island has twelve parishes, each enjoying their own little bit of the dramatic coastline, and the main resort and the 'city' of Jersey is St Helier. St Helier's waterfront, formerly a dreary area of commercial wharfs and ferry terminals dominated by a power station, continues to undergo a massive refurbishment. There are many new public spaces, fountains and facilities being created. The attractive buildings housing the Occupation Tapestry and Maritime Museum are a good start. Across the sweeping, sheltered bay of St Aubin is Elizabeth Castle, a Tudor fortress, romantically floodlit at night.

Liberation Square, focus of post-World War II jubilation (notice the bronze sculpture of flag-waving revellers), makes a natural starting point. Nearby is the colourful **Steam Clock**. In the streets behind you'll discover the town's true character – quaint old shop-fronts and names in Norman French. Visit the delightful old market and historic **Royal Square**, where one of the Commonwealth's oldest parliaments sits. Though densely populated, St Helier has its quieter side. The immaculate gardens of **Howard Davis Park** offer a peaceful retreat from traffic fumes.

> Several of Jersey's best museums, run by the Jersey Museums Service, have a combined ticketing scheme – excellent value if you visit more than a couple. Passport Savers can be purchased at any participating ticket office or from your holiday representative.

THINGS TO SEE & DO
Jersey Museum ★★★
An award-winning multi-media presentation of Jersey's history and culture, with an art gallery and excellent catering facilities. Interesting

sections on Lillie Langtry (Edward VII's glamorous mistress), and a restored merchant's house on the top floor. ⓐ The Weighbridge ① 01534 633 300 ⓛ Open 10.00–17.00 (summer and mid-Mar–Oct); 10.00–16.00 (winter) ❶ Admission charge

Elizabeth Castle ★ ★ ★

The unmissable causeway fortress in St Aubin's Bay dates from the 1590s, and was named after Elizabeth I. It houses history exhibitions and the Royal Jersey Militia Museum. Access on foot (low tide only) or by an

🔻 *Elizabeth Castle, linked by a causeway to the mainland*

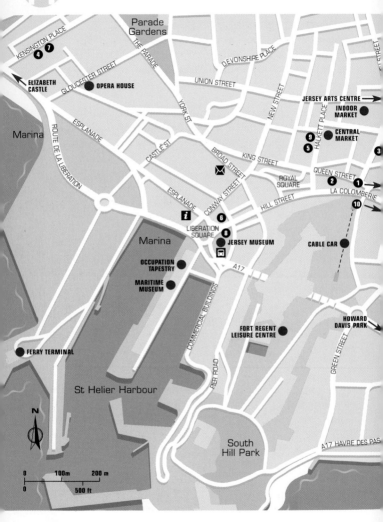

amphibious vehicle dubbed the 'duck' (extra charge). Behind the castle is the Hermitage, a 12th-century chapel dedicated to St Helier, who was murdered by axe-wielding pirates. Difficult access for disabled visitors. ⓐ St Aubin's Bay ❶ 01534 633 300 ⓛ Open 10.00–18.00 (mid-Mar–Oct) ❶ Admission charge

Occupation Tapestry ★★★

An ambitious project, the Occupation Tapestry was completed in 1995 and involved the whole island. It contains over seven million stitches. The tapestry was made to commemorate the 50th anniversary of the Liberation and each parish contributed one of the dozen panels depicting Jersey's wartime experiences. Informative video and gift shop. ⓐ New North Quay ❶ 01534 811 043 ⓛ Open 10.00–17.00 (summer and mid Mar–Oct); 10.00–16.00 (winter) ❶ Admission charge

Maritime Museum ★★★

In the same attractive, modern, waterfront premises as the Occupation Tapestry, this excellent museum has many entertaining 'hands-on' ways to learn about tides, winds, cleats and sails. A must for sailing enthusiasts. ⓐ New North Quay ❶ 01534 811 043 ⓛ Open 10.00–17.00 (summer and mid Mar–-Oct); 10.00–16.00 (winter) ❶ Admission charge

Fort Regent Leisure Centre ★★

The curious golf ball structure towering over St Helier's harbour houses a massive sports, leisure and entertainment complex in the grounds of a 19th-century fort. Has a 2,000 seater concert hall. Learn the history of the fort on a guided tour, and don't miss the signalling tower and the rampart views. ⓐ Fort Regent ❶ 01534 500 200 ⓛ Opening times vary according to activity or event ❶ Admission free, pay as you play

RESTAURANTS & PUBS (see map opposite)

As you might expect, St Helier has the island's widest choice of eating and drinking venues, including chain restaurants such as Pizza Express and McDonald's. Several pubs offer regular live music in the evenings.

The Admiral Wine & Ale House £ ❶ One of St Helier's best-known haunts for inexpensive lunchtime food, decent bitter and dominoes. ⓐ 12–14 St James Street ⓣ 01534 730 095 ⓛ Open daily; evening meals from 18.00

La Bastille Taverne £ ❷ Popular daytime restaurant-wine bar serving a wide range of dishes at very reasonable prices. Daily specials and good seafood. ⓐ 45 Queen Street ⓣ 01534 874 059 ⓛ Open Mon–Sat noon–16.00

Blue Fish Café ££ ❸ This trendy, informal eatery in central St Helier specialises in pasta, pizza and brochettes. There is outdoor seating during summer, and it is cosy in winter. ⓐ West Centre ⓣ 01534 767 186 ⓘ Popular, so book in advance

Candlelight Restaurant ££ ❹ This restaurant, which is part of a 17th-century coach house that is now the Revere Hotel, serves French and English cuisine in traditional surroundings. Fine wines are featured, and it is within walking distance of the Esplanade. ⓐ Kensington Place ⓣ 01534 611 111

La Capannina £££ ❺ An accomplished Italian restaurant, highly acclaimed for traditional cuisine using local produce, as well as its quality wine list. ⓐ 65–67 Halkett Place ⓣ 01534 734 602 ⓛ Open Mon–Sat ⓘ Smart and formal – book ahead

Chambers £ ❻ A younger sibling of the long-established Admiral, this popular pub appeals to a lively crowd, with regular music in the evenings. It has well-kept beers and good-value bar food. ⓐ Mulcaster Street ⓣ 01534 880 432

ⓞ *The intricate commemorative Occupation Tapestry (see page 71)*

🔺 *Jersey Opera House*

🍴 **Doran's Courtyard Bistro** ££ ❼ An intimate ambience of warehouse windows, rustic beams and flagstone floors adds to the imaginative, eclectic fare served here. As to be expected, it is very popular with locals. 🅰 Kensington Place ☎ 01534 734 866 🕐 Open Mon–Sat ❗ Book ahead

☕ **Jersey Museum Brasserie** £ ❽ This excellent place is open to non-museum visitors and serves sophisticated snacks and cakes. 🅰 The Weighbridge ☎ 01534 510 069 🕐 Open museum hours and for evening dining from 18.30

🍴 **KG's Diner** £ ❾ A clean, comfortable, welcoming place to enjoy some of Jersey's best fish and chips, plus great steaks and snacks. Good value, friendly service and wines by the glass. 🅰 Opposite Jersey Library, 90–92 Halkett Place ☎ 01534 721 395

🍴 **Olive Branch** ££ ❿ An eclectic menu includes homemade pastas and the finest Italian sauces. Good wine list with a plentiful

number of Italian wines. Light, modern decor and friendly staff. 🅐 35–39
La Colomberie 🕐 Open Mon–Sat 🕿 01534 615 993

NIGHTLIFE

Despite its size, Jersey has a wide range of entertainment. Much of it
centres on St Helier, where pubs and clubs keep going until the small
hours. In particular, the area surrounding the bus station is where many
nightlife venues can be found. Check the *Jersey Evening Post* for the
latest events. Nightlife tends to be busiest during the summer months.
You can choose from a military band playing in Howard Davis Park to a
rock band in **Chambers Pub** or a jazz trio in the **Blue Note Bar**.

If your tastes are more high-brow, see what is on at the **Jersey Opera
House**. This newly restored 600-seat theatre in Gloucester Street holds
performances every week of touring musicals and plays. Also check out
the **Jersey Arts Centre**, a smaller theatre hosting classical recitals, plays
and art exhibitions. Jersey has two cinemas in town; the **Odeon** in Bath
Street is the largest and shows the latest releases.

Outside St Helier, nightlife is rather quieter. At **Wolf's Caves** in St
John, the **Jersey Country Music Club** meets weekly. If you want something different, you can join in with Latin, Ballroom, sequence and
Egyptian dance classes. Some hotels, including the **Merton** and **Hotel
de Normandie**, provide entertainment open to non-residents.

A SHORT HOP TO FRANCE

Guernsey is an easy hop to France. **St Malo** is a delightful place for
a day out. Walk round the ramparts and have a good lunch. From
here, it's possible to reach the elegant seaside resort of **Dinard** on
the opposite side of the Rance (visit the amazing Tidal Barrage on
the way). Upstream, you'll find the gorgeous old town of **Dinan**,
and 45 minutes' drive to the east the magical abbey fortress of
Mont St Michel rises like a mirage from the bay. Don't forget to
take your passport!

Southern tour, Jersey
day trip from St Peter to Grouville

St Peter is first landfall for most visitors to Jersey – the island's airport is here. St Brelade, in the south-western corner, is one of the best-known and best-loved of Jersey's parishes. St Brelade's Bay is the island's most attractive beach resort, basking amid palm-fringed gardens. It boasts of being the most southerly seaside town in the British Isles – a claim occasionally challenged by St Helier.

Though somewhat suburban in parts, both parishes have surprising swathes of unspoilt greenery. St Peter's Valley is one of Jersey's prettiest and greenest drives. With two separate stretches of coastline, St Peter offers access to Jersey's largest beaches and a variety of water sports facilities. St Brelade's capitalises on one of Jersey's best family beaches. Glorious peaceful coves nestle between rocky headlands to either side, and rare wildlife haunts the open spaces behind. Beyond the fortified promontory of Noirmont, St Aubin has a distinctive salty character and is home to the prestigious Royal Channel Island Yacht Club.

Next are the parishes of St Lawrence and St Saviour. You'll certainly find yourself travelling through these central parishes at some stage. They suffer rather from their proximity to St Helier, with busy traffic routes and built-up areas, but inland these are soon outstripped. St Lawrence has several interesting sights. The huge bay of St Aubin's is a fine, firm crescent of sand, if rather spoilt by the busy highway running directly behind.

Two of the most interesting attractions in St Lawrence are the **German Underground Hospital**, an amazing complex of underground tunnels constructed in the last war, and the **Hamptonne Country Life Museum**, run by the Jersey Museums Service and occupying one of the finest farmhouses in the parish. As you drive around, you'll see other impressive examples of Jersey's vernacular domestic architecture too. Several of these are looked after by the National Trust for Jersey (though not open to the public). Look out for **Morel Farm** and **Le Rat Cottage**.

◬ *St Brelade's Bay*

A couple of churches are worth visiting too: **Millbrook's Glass Church** is decorated with astonishing Lalique glasswork, like sculpted ice, while **St Saviour's church** is the last resting place of the dashing Emilie Charlotte le Breton, better known as Lillie Langtry. Nearby, have a look at the imposing residence of the Lieutenant Governor, the Queen's representative on Jersey.

St Clement and Grouville are different again. Once free of St Helier's suburban tentacles, the hinterland of these southern parishes consists of open farmland and proper villages boasting rustic inns and churches. Take a drive along the coastal road past **St Clement's Bay** at low tide to see a strange lunar seascape of exposed reefs and rocks. It's particularly dramatic in morning light, so bring your camera. There are free parking places at intervals. Take care if you walk along the beach – the incoming tide moves extremely fast and can be dangerous.

THINGS TO SEE & DO
Fisherman's Chapel ★★
The stippled frescoes in the early Norman chapel behind St Brelade's Bay look as though some agile leopard has had a shot at wall-painting with its paws. ⓐ St Brelade's Bay ❶ Donations welcome

German Underground Hospital ★★★
This graphic evocation of the Occupation period is set in a complex of tunnels dug by forced labour and equipped as a hospital for German casualties. It includes fascinating reconstructions and film footage. ⓐ Meadowback, St Lawrence ❶ 01534 863 442 ● Open 10.00–18.00 (Feb–Dec) ❶ Admission charge

Hamptonne Country Life Museum ★★
An enjoyable folk museum comprising reconstructions of Jersey rural scenes, craft demonstrations, a nature trail and farm animals. Periodic special events. ⓐ La Rue de la Patente, St Lawrence ❶ 01534 863 955 ● Open daily 10.00–17.00 (April–Oct) ❶ Admission charge

Jersey Goldsmiths ★★
This widely promoted attraction is featured on many sightseeing tours. You can watch craftsmen at work, and investigate a huge range of costume jewellery, much of it plated in 18-carat gold. Repairs and adjustments are also carried out, and there is a garden terrace restaurant. ⓐ Lion Park, in the heart of the island in the St Lawrence parish, Five Mile Road, St Ouen ❶ 01534 482 098 ● Open 10.00–17.00 ❶ Admission free

Jersey Lavender Farm ★★
Lavender is grown and harvested on the farm, and the oil is then extracted and blended into cosmetics and toiletries. Visit the farm, the distillery and, of course, the shop. There is is also a video presentation. A good time to visit is in June when the harvest begins. ⓐ Rue du Pont Marquet, St Brelade ❶ 01534 742 933 ● Open Tues–Sun 10.00–17.00 (May–Sept) ❶ Admission charge

🔺 *Visit Jersey Lavender Farm for the wonderful scents*

Jersey Motor Museum ★

Contains veteran and vintage cars, and a section on Jersey's steam railway. **ⓐ** St Peter's Village **ⓣ** 01534 482 966 **ⓛ** Open 10.00–17.00 (April–Oct) **ⓘ** Admission charge

Jersey Pottery ★★★

This successful family-run pottery makes a thoroughly enjoyable excursion. Visitors may watch its charming, handmade ceramics being thrown, fired and painted by skilled artists. A showroom displays the results, and there's no pressure to buy. Other on-site attractions include the Glaze Craze, which allows you to have a go at painting your own design, and splendid brasseries and restaurants. The pottery stands in lovely gardens. **ⓐ** Gorey Village **ⓣ** 01534 851 119 **ⓛ** Showroom open Mon–Sat 09.00–17.30, Sun 10.00–17.30; no production on Sat and Sun **ⓘ** Admission free

The Glass Church ★★

This intriguing church contains remarkable moulded white glass by the French artist René Lalique. **ⓐ** Millbrook, St Lawrence, near Coronation Park **ⓣ** 01534 502 864 **ⓛ** Open Sun–Fri 09.00–18.00 (summer) and 09.00–dusk (winter) **ⓘ** Donation welcome

La Hougue Bie ★★

Deep in rural seclusion stands a 12 m (40 ft) mound pierced by a mysterious passage entrance. It's a Neolithic burial site dating back over five

🔺 *The Glass Church*

thousand years. Later ages added medieval chapels and a German underground bunker. A visitor centre interprets the site simply and accessibly, paying particular attention to children. ❷ Route de la Hougue Bie, Grouville ❶ 01534 853 823 ❸ Open 10.00–17.00 (Mar–Oct) ❶ Admission charge

The Living Legend ★★★

One of Jersey's foremost attractions, The Living Legend incorporates a multi-media presentation of the island's story (The Jersey Experience) with lots of special effects. Standing within the same complex of landscaped grounds and play areas is adventure golf, a craft and shopping village, a restaurant, an ice-cream parlour and a fudge factory. ❷ La Rue du Petit Aleval, St Peter ❶ 01534 485 496 ❸ Open daily 09.30–17.00 (April–Oct), Sat–Wed 10.00–17.00 (Mar and Nov) ❶ Admission charge

● *La Hougue Bie, the neolithic burial site*

Le Moulin de Quétivel ★★

See the mill wheel in action at this well-restored 18th century watermill owned by Jersey National Trust. There is also stone-ground flour for sale, and a herb garden. ❷ Mont Fallu, St Peter ❶ 01534 745 408 ❸ Open Tues–Thurs 10.00–16.00 (May–Sept) ❶ Admission charge (free to worldwide National Trust members)

Samarès Manor ★★★

This Norman seigneurial manor supplements its visitor attractions with a magnificent herb garden and plant nursery, crafts centre, tea gardens and fun farm. Demonstrations of woodturning and falconry are available, as well as guided tours of the house and the agricultural and carriage museum. ⓐ Inner Road, St Clement ❶ 01534 870 551 ⓛ Open Mon–Sat 10.00–17.00; tours of house Mon–Sat (additional charge); free garden talks Mon–Fri afternoons (Mar–Oct) ❶ Admission charge

RESTAURANTS & PUBS

Jersey's southern coast rejoices in several superb restaurants with moderate prices. It's worth working up an appetite if you're heading in this direction.

⬣ Old Portelet Inn

Borsalino Rocque ££ A large, popular place, smart but friendly, with a huge menu. Lunches are moderate; dinners pricier. Disco dancing some evenings. ⓐ La Grande Route des Sablons, Grouville ⓣ 01534 852 111 ⓛ Open Wed–Mon for lunch and evening meal ❶ Book ahead for the conservatory

British Union £ This popular roadside pub serves simple bar food and offers pleasant service, a games room and a playhouse. ⓐ Main Road, St Lawrence, in the centre of the island ⓣ 01534 861 070 ⓛ Open daily for lunch and evening meals (except Sun)

Green Island ££ This low-key place occupies a prime location overlooking the dramatic reef-strewn coastline of St Clement's Bay. The simple interior and modest price tags disguise some very interesting cooking (the owner is a celebrated Jersey restaurateur). There are also inexpensive takeaways and snacks, as well as terrace tables and free parking. ⓐ Green Island, St Clement's Bay ⓣ 01534 857 787 ⓛ Open Tues–Sat for lunch and evening meals, and Sun lunchtime

Jersey Pottery Restaurants £–£££ After much-deserved praise in several top food guides, these restaurants are now just as prestigious as the pottery. Outstanding cooking uses quality produce and local fish. The Garden Restaurant, Spinnakers Bar and Grill and the gastro bar, Castle Green, offer excellent value. ⓐ Gorey Village, Grouville ⓣ 01534 851 119 ⓛ Open daily 09.00–17.30 and evenings in the summer

Longueville Manor £££ One of Jersey's most august and celebrated restaurants in a country house hotel. Smart and formal but very comfortable, with a courteous, welcoming service. Fine gastronomy menus using homegrown fruit, vegetables and herbs. Vegetarian options. ⓐ Longueville Road, St Saviour ⓣ 01534 725 501

Ming's Dynasty ££ There are three branches of this popular Chinese restaurant on Jersey, all producing reliable, well-prepared oriental classics, incorporating fresh local seafood. ⓐ Sandybrook Lane, St Lawrence ⓣ 01534 888 682 ⓛ Open at 18.00

Old Court House Inn ££ A fine historic building on the harbour front, as popular for its characterful interior and friendly service as for its excellent food and ales. Several bars and dining rooms offer varied menus and ambience. You may remember it as a well-used back-drop to the 1980s *Bergerac* TV detective series. ⓐ St Aubin's Harbour, St Brelade ⓣ 01534 746 433 ⓛ Open for lunch and evening meals

Old Portelet Inn £ An excellent place for families, this dashingly converted farmhouse inn occupies a splendid location above Portelet Bay. Great-value bar food and well-kept ales. Tables outside; music some evenings, and friendly service. ⓐ Portelet, St Brelade ⓣ 01534 741 899 ⓛ Open Tues–Sun for lunch and evening meals

Pembroke £ This welcoming pub draws both visitors and locals for its friendly family atmosphere and good-value food at lunchtime and in the evenings. ⓐ Grouville Coast Road, Grouville ⓣ 01534 855 756 ⓛ Open daily all year

Smugglers Inn £ Down by the beach at Ouaisne, this traditional family pub serves wholesome lunches and dinners, popular after a day on the beach. ⓐ Ouaisne, St Brelade ⓣ 01534 741 510 ⓛ Open for lunch and evening meals (except Sun evening in winter)

Secret Garden £ A popular daytime stop for cream teas and lunches. A licensed restaurant, it has daily specials and family favourites like lasagne and jacket potatoes. Seafood is a speciality. There is a cottage-style interior, tables outside on fine days, and a walled garden. ⓐ Gorey Common, Grouville ⓣ 01534 852 999 ⓛ Open Wed–Mon 11.00–22.00 for late breakfast, lunch and evening meals (summer)

The Hamptonne Café £ The Country Life Museum's attractive café will organise a picnic for you to eat in the meadow, or snacks and teas throughout the day. Typical Jersey recipes are served. ⓐ La Rue de la Patente, St Lawrence ❶ 01534 862 698 ❶ Open April–Oct

The Star £ A friendly village pub offering terrific value. Locals and families mingle happily here with visitors. No food is served at present although possible plans include an Oriental-style restaurant. ⓐ St Peter's Village ❶ 01534 485 556

Village Bistro ££ An innovative menu that has become known on Jersey's gastronomic scene. Local produce is used to good effect in appetising modern dishes. Set menus represent excellent value. ⓐ Gorey Village, Grouville ❶ 01534 853 429 ❶ Open Tues–Sat for lunch and evening meals, and Sun lunchtimes

Victoria Pub £ Popular family pub in the rural centre of the island. ⓐ St Peter's Valley ❶ 01534 485 498 ❶ Open Tues–Sat for lunch and evening meals, plus Sun lunchtime for traditional roasts

Zanzibar ££ A stylish beach bistro with a fabulous veranda view of St Brelade's Bay. Cosmopolitan cooking

● *The Victoria Pub, in rural St Peter's Valley*

and colonial décor give this lively, informal place a sophisticated air. ⓐ St Brelade's Bay, St Brelade ❶ 01534 741 081 ❶ Open Tues–Sat for lunch and evening meal, and Sun lunchtime

85

Northern tour, Jersey
day trip from St Mary to St Martin

The northern coast of Jersey is easily accessible from Guernsey. Cliff paths stretch along the scenic northern headlands through the parishes of St Mary and St John, offering beautiful but taxing walks. There isn't much sand between Bonne Nuit Bay and Grève de Lecq, but energetic walkers can explore many minor natural features, such as the Wolf's Caves or the Devil's Hole. Take care with cliffs and tides and watch out for warning signs.

This rugged coastline is best explored on foot, as the roads do not run by the sea. Some is National Trust land. A blaze of wildflowers can be seen in spring and summer and the area is a haunt of rare birds. It isn't always quiet, though: isolated headlands sometimes reverberate to the sounds of motorcycle scrambling or rifle shooting, and there are seasonal flickers of nightlife if you are out after hours at Grève de Lecq and Wolf's Caves.

There are a few small prehistoric sites, including tumuli dating from around 3500 BC. **L'Ile Agois** was once an islet hermitage, and can be reached at low tide. The hinterland is quiet and agricultural, scattered with fine examples of domestic architecture. For more information on this part of the island it is a good idea to visit the **North Coast Visitor Centre**, housed in the Napoleonic barracks at Grève de Lecq.

You can have a closer look at some of Jersey's most traditional farmhouses by visiting tourist attractions such as **La Mare Vineyards** or the **Jersey Butterfly Farm**. Another fine building called **The Elms** is headquarters of the Jersey National Trust. Most imposing of all is **St John's Manor**, a classically proportioned house open occasionally for charity events.

Jersey's northeastern parishes of Trinity and St Martin encompass the island's highest point, and some of its prettiest and most rural scenery. North of Gorey stretches a series of quiet, sandy bays, safe and unpolluted. Along the rugged northern shore, cliffs soar to a height of

◐ *Jersey's dramatic north coast, view towards Sorel*

⬥ *The popular family beach at Grève de Lecq*

120 m (400 ft) above the picturesque fishing harbours of **Rozel** and **Bouley Bay**. Inland, a spider's web of secretive country lanes conceals dignified, prosperous-looking farmsteads.

One of these, **Les Augrès Manor**, now hosts the world-famous zoo, set up by the late Gerald Durrell. Other popular sights in this part of Jersey include **Mont Orgeuil Castle** in Gorey, and the exotic and riotously colourful blooms of the **Eric Young Orchid Foundation**. The massive breakwater at **St Catherine's Bay** also provides a pier that is popular with amateur fishermen.

More ominous is the rocky outcrop called **Geoffrey's Leap**, where condemned criminals plunged to their enforced deaths in medieval times. The steep slopes behind Bouley Bay are the scene of an annual motorised hill-climbing championship.

The quiet reservoir of Queen's Valley, inland from Gorey, is also a nature reserve. The pathways leading round its edges make a gentle 1 km (2 mile) stroll. Take a picnic with you, or combine a walk with a visit to the nearby Jersey Pottery and its excellent brasserie/restaurant. There are additional car parks at either end of the reservoir.

THINGS TO SEE & DO
Eric Young Orchid Foundation ★★
Green-fingered visitors beat a path through tiny lanes to these exotic hothouses where the lifetime's work of an orchid addict can be seen. High summer is not the best time to visit, but there are gorgeous flowers all year round in an astonishing range of shapes and colours. A wonderful experience. ⓐ Victoria Village, Trinity ⓣ 01534 861 963 ⓛ Open Wed–Sat 10.00–16.00 (all year) ⓘ Admission charge

Gorey Village ★★
The picturesque cluster of harbour cottages dwarfed by Jersey's oldest castle makes a classic photo opportunity. Besides excellent restaurants, shops, crafts and pubs, Gorey boasts several first-rate sights and overlooks a magnificent beach. More good beaches and pretty countryside lie nearby. Needless to say, it's popular in high season.

Pallot Heritage Steam Museum ★
Steam engines, farm machinery, theatre organs and other bygones. Occasional steam train rides and special events. ⓐ Rue de Bechet, Trinity ⓣ 01534 865 307 ⓛ Open Mon–Sat 10.00–17.00 (April–Oct) ⓘ Admission charge

Little Loft Gallery & Turnery ★
Mick Renouf's beautifully hand-turned vases, bowls and goblets, made mostly from native hardwoods, are displayed in this farmhouse gallery. ⓐ Brabant Farm, Rue de Brabant, Trinity ⓣ 01534 863 674 ⓛ Open by appointment only ⓘ Admission free

La Mare Vineyards ★

These are Jersey's only commercial vineyards, planted in 1972 in the grounds of a fine 18th-century farmhouse. They produce in the region of 40,000 bottles of wine per season, along with its renowned cider and calvados apple brandy. La Mare also produces preserves, mustards, fudge, traditional black butter and chocolates in its estate kitchens. There are video and exhibitions, as well as tastings and produce on sale, and an adventure playground for the children. ⓐ St Mary ⓣ 01534 481 178 ⓛ Open Mon–Sat 10.00–17.00 (Mar–Oct) ⓘ Admission charge

Jersey Zoo ★★★

The late Gerald Durrell's imaginative sanctuary and breeding centre has won many awards for its ground-breaking contribution to wildlife conservation. Rare species are rescued from the brink of extinction, and reintroduced to the wild. An informative, entertaining and inspiring place with a friendly, direct approach to visitors. The Café Dodo is a good bet for lunch or afternoon tea. ⓐ Les Augrès Manor, Trinity ⓣ 01534 860 000 ⓛ Open 09.30–18.00 (summer), 10.00–17.00 (winter, except Christmas Day) ⓘ Admission charge

Mont Orgeuil Castle ★★★

This splendid fortress, with lovely rampart views, has dominated Grouville Bay and Gorey Village since the 13th century, and is in remarkable condition. Exhibitions inside recount its history. ⓐ Gorey, St Martin ⓣ 01534 853 292 ⓛ Open daily 10.00–18.00 (Mar–Oct), weekends only (winter) ⓘ Admission charge

North Coast Visitor Centre ★

Housed in the neat, symmetrical buildings of a 19th-century Napoleonic-era barracks, this National Trust-owned visitor centre has displays and literature on local history, footpaths, wildlife, etc. ⓐ Grève de Lecq, St Mary ⓣ 01534 483 193 ⓛ Open Tues–Sat 11.00–17.00, Sun 14.00–17.00 (May–Sept) ⓘ Admission free

⬥ *Jersey's green lanes invite exploration*

RESTAURANTS & PUBS

There's some wonderful fine dining to be had along the north coast, along with good value snacks in pubs and teashops.

The Buttery Restaurant and Tearooms £ The tea rooms attached to La Mare Vineyards are pleasant for a snack, with home-baked cakes and tables in the garden in fine weather. You may be able to taste some home produce here, including cider or perhaps even calvados (apple brandy). ⓐ Rue de la Hougue Mauger, St Mary ❶ 01534 481 178 ❶ Open Mon–Sat 10.00–17.00 (Mar–Oct) ❶ Admission charge

Chateau La Chaire £££ This luxury hotel-restaurant occupies a beautiful secluded spot near the island's tip. An elegant place, so book ahead and dress up. Cooking is ambitious 'modern British', and very fishy. The oak-panelled restaurant has a conservatory extension. Dining on the terrace in summer. ⓐ Rozel Bay, St Martin ❶ 01534 863 354

Drive Inn BBQ £ Popular with families for its generous helpings of chargrilled meat and fish served on a flower-decked terrace or in Western-style wagons. Self-service salad bar – eat as much as you like. ⓐ Gorey Coast Road, St Martin ❶ 01534 851 266 ❶ Open May–Sept

Les Fontaines Tavern £ Location is one of this old granite pub's selling points; it has spectacular ocean views. Inside, it has lots of character – inglenooks, ship's timber beams and an ancient cider press. Randall's ales and inexpensive bar food served at lunchtime and dinner. ⓐ Route du Nord, St John ❶ 01534 862 707 ❶ Open 11.00–23.00 ❶ Children's play area

Le Frere Restaurant £££ Sitting at the top of Rozel Bay, the 'Frere' is a seafood haven, perfect for special occasion meals. Booking required. ⓐ Rozel Bay, St Martin ❶ 01534 861 000 ❶ Open Tues–Sun for lunch, and Tues–Sat for evening meals

Gardener's Tearoom and Restaurant £ Good wholesome family food served in the courtyard during the summer. Dishes such as local fish, pasta and exotic salads are prepared fresh on the premises. Delicious homemade cakes, bread and cream teas are also available. ☎ 01534 853 668 🕒 Open Tues–Sun for lunch

Royal St Martin £ Renowned for its excellent bar food, this land-mark village pub in the centre of St Martin also has a separate restaurant. Good real ales. Families welcome. ⊜ Grande Route de Faldouet, St Martin ☎ 01534 851 098 🕒 Open daily for lunch, and Mon–Sat for evening meals

Rozel Bay and Upstairs Restaurant £ This cosy seaside pub serves much-acclaimed food, especially fish. Lunchtime fare is more traditional and less expensive, but the dinner fare is exceptional. There are gardens and pub games available. ⊜ Rozel Bay, St Martin ☎ 01534 863 438 ❗ Booking is recommended in high season; children are welcome

St Mary's Country Inn £ One of the best examples of a Jersey speciality – the family-friendly country pub. Civilised and welcoming, this inn offers a hearty range of lunchtime and evening food. Family conservatory room (no smoking) and tables outside for al fresco summer dining. ⊜ St Mary ☎ 01534 481 561 🕒 Open 10.00–23.30

Suma's ££ This attractive venture offers discerning palates a chance to try first-class cooking at affordable prices. Under the same management as Longueville Manor, Suma's has an airy upstairs dining-room, simple but stylish, overlooking Gorey Harbour. Good-value set lunches. They also feature an in-house bakery and a good wine list. ⊜ Gorey Hill, St Martin ☎ 01534 853 291 🕒 Open daily ❗ Children welcome

EXCURSIONS

St Ouen, Jersey
blooms and beaches tour

St Ouen (pronounced 'won') is Jersey's largest parish. It makes up the north-western corner of the island, and is a varied and beautiful stretch of striking coastline and quiet farmland. Much is still uncultivated, making it a good place for walkers and nature-lovers. Coastal paths follow most of the shore, partly on breezy clifftops, partly beside peaceful dunes. There are some dangers on this exposed Atlantic seaboard, so it is wise to watch out for warning signs.

St Ouen boasts a large number of visitor attractions, although few merit more than a 'see if passing' rating. Many are clustered around L'Etacq and St Ouen's Bay, and most craft showrooms are free of charge. If you're keen on wildlife, visit the **Kempt Tower** and **Francis Le Sueur Centre** to learn more about Jersey's flora and fauna, or perhaps take in a guided nature walk through the reedbeds and lagoons behind St Ouen's Bay.

Grève de Lecq and **Plémont Bay** are two of Jersey's most appealing smaller beaches, while the giant, 8 km (5 mile) strand of St Ouen's Bay attracts surfers. Inland, the manor and church of St Ouen hark back to feudal times.

It's tempting to put your foot down if you are driving on the long straight road behind St Ouen's Bay. **La Route des Mielles** is one of the few stretches on Jersey where this is possible. Be careful if you're walking across this road – especially with young children. If you are driving, remember the island's speed limit is only 65 kph (40 mph).

THINGS TO SEE & DO
Battle of Flowers Museum ★
A display of floats from Jersey's colourful annual parade, which usually takes place in August. Many of the award-winning floats were hand-made by museum founder Florence Bechelet. Taped commentary is available. ⓐ Mont des Corvées, St Ouen ⓣ 01534 482 408 ⓛ Open 10.00–17.00 (Easter–Oct) ⓘ Admission charge

94

◆ *Windsurfing at St Ouen's Bay*

Bouchet Agateware Pottery ★

A unique and secret process developed by founder Tony Bouchet lies behind the production of the stunning marbled ceramic pieces produced in this tiny pottery. Visit the showroom and find out more. ⓐ Rue des Marettes, St Ouen ❶ 01534 482 345 ❶ Open 09.00 17.00 (limited opening times in winter) ❶ Admission free

Jersey Pearl ★

Simulated and cultured pearl jewellery is on show (and on sale) here, alongside other precious and semi-precious gems and watches. Find out what the largest pearl in the world looks like. There are workshop demonstrations and exhibitions as well as tea rooms and gift shops. ⓐ North End Five Mile Road, St Ouen (also at Jersey airport and Gorey Pier shop) ❶ 01534 862 137 ❶ Open 10.00–17.30 (summer), 10.00–16.30 (winter); ❶ Admission free

Kempt Tower ★

The stumpy Martello Tower at the north end of St Ouen's Bay houses a
visitor centre and a video theatre dedicated to Jersey's natural history.
Relevant literature is on sale. Nearby are the **Frances Le Sueur Centre**
(another environmental information point) and **Les Mielles**, a nature
reserve. ⓐ St Ouen's Bay ⓣ 01534 483 651 ⓛ Open Tues–Sun
14.00–17.00 (April–Oct); free guided nature walks on Thursdays
in summer ⓘ Admission free

PICNIC SPOTS

The clifftop walk between Grève de Lecq and L'Etacq leads past some
panoramic views. **Plémont Point** is a good spot for birdwatching: auks,
fulmars and shags nest on the cliffs, while pipits and linnets flit across
the open heathland behind. On a fine day, the 14th-century ruins of
Grosnez Castle, 60 m (200 ft) above sea level, make a scenic vantage
point. Further round the headland, **Le Pinacle** is a rock spire by the
water's edge. A sea cave is exposed at low tide. Wild flowers carpet
the treeless expanses of **Les Landes** in spring.

RESTAURANTS

Moulin de Lecq £ The watermill theme of this delightful place
makes it instantly appealing; you can see the machinery gears
turning as you order drinks at the bar. Log fires, real ales and generous
bar food add to its immense olde worlde character. A large new restaurant
opened in 2006. There is a children's playground and al fresco dining
in the summer. ⓐ Grève de Lecq, St Ouen ⓣ 01534 482 818
ⓛ Open for lunch and evening meals

The Snow Goose £ This pleasant daytime tea room opposite
the parish hall serves morning coffee, light lunches and cream
teas. Attached is a large display of gifts and crafts. ⓐ St Ouen village
ⓣ 01534 484 404 ⓛ Open daily 10.00–17.00 (summer); Tues–Sat
10.00–17.00 (winter)

Food & drink

EATING OUT

Unlike the unfortunate islanders who endured wartime occupation on grisly fare like parsnip coffee and peapod tea, today's holidaymakers can expect good rations. Eating is an important part of life in Guernsey and its islands. Local ingredients, especially seafood, market garden vegetables and dairy produce, are renowned for their freshness and quality. But many staples have to be imported, so the cost of eating out, or shopping for self-catering, may be higher than you expect.

> Tourist Information Centres' eating out guides give useful restaurant suggestions, although they don't always list the more exclusive eating places. If you prefer to eat and drink without a garnish of cigarette ash, pick up the smoke-free guide to Channel Island pubs and restaurants.

BUDGET EATING

Excellent and imaginative cooking can still be had at moderate prices in Guernsey, with many tourist restaurants remaining heartily traditional. Whatever the map suggests, culinary styles are closer to England than to France. Croissants and baguettes are on sale in the bakeries, but you're more likely to find a classic British fry-up on your hotel breakfast plate. At Sunday lunchtimes, traditional carvery roasts are always popular.

Dozens of friendly, family-oriented pubs offer well-tried favourites like ploughman's lunches and chilli con carne, though these aren't the only things on bar menus. There's no shortage of cafés for cream teas, fish-and-chip shops for filling takeaways, and Indian, Chinese or Italian restaurants to provide reliable, inexpensive solutions to hunger pangs.

SEAFOOD

Finned or shelled, fish dishes feature on nearly every island menu. In the fast, tidal waters surrounding the Channel Islands, pollution levels are

THE ORMER

The mysterious ormer, a large mollusc like an asymmetrical limpet, derives its name from the French 'oreille de mer' (sea ear).

The Channel Islands are the northern limit of its habitat, yet this local delicacy is now rare due to over-fishing. As such, strict regulations apply to the collection of ormers. They must only be harvested between the months of September and April, and only on the first day of the full moon and for the three days after. During this period, Guernsey men and women scour the rocks to find the sought-after ormer. These rules are strictly policed and heavy fines are levied on offenders.

Once found, the ormer is prised from the underside of rocks by hand and carried to shore in a traditional ormer basket. It is then beaten and cooked in the oven as a casserole or served with gravy, carrots and onions. The ormer's striking mother-of-pearl inner shell is also used as decoration on houses and for jewellery.

much lower than in some holiday destinations, so eating shellfish is less like playing Russian roulette with your stomach. Besides crab, brill and sea-bass, look out for Sark lobster and Herm oysters.

In the Channel Islands, humble British fish and chips attains classic status, but you will also find more elaborate French-style dishes like those popular in nearby Brittany and Normandy. Conger eel soup is a local favourite. Some expensive kinds of seafood, such as spider crab, are sold by weight rather than by portion. Check carefully when you order, to avoid a nasty shock when you receive the bill.

FRUIT & VEGETABLES

Huge acreages of Guernsey are under glass, which produces some wonderful fruit and vegetables, although crops have altered in line with commercial pressures. Tomatoes, ousted by subsidised foreign

🔺 *Succulent Chancre crab for sale*

competition, have often given way to flowers. Market gardening is still important, however. Jersey Royal new potatoes, boiled and buttered with herbs, are certainly a dish fit for a queen or a king.

Strawberries, celery, courgettes and many salad crops are raised for local consumption as well as the export trade. You'll often see produce on sale in little hatches by the roadsides, accompanied by an honesty box to leave money in.

DAIRY PRODUCE

Most people are aware of Channel Island 'gold top' milk, with its high butterfat content. Butter and cream are produced in huge quantities, enriching local menus everywhere. Apart from a little Guernsey cheddar, you won't see much island-produced cheese – the milk sours too quickly.

CAKES

All kinds of cakes and scones appear in the islands' tea gardens and coffee shops. For something local, look out for *fiottes* (balls of sweet pastry) and Guernsey *gâche* (pronounced 'gosh') which is a fruit tea bread. You can sometimes buy this ready buttered by the slice. Try the bakeries in St Peter Port or St Sampson. Also look out for Jersey Wonders (a kind of doughnut) and don't forget to try some Channel Island fudge; it's available in an amazing range of flavours.

TRADITIONAL DISHES

One country recipe widely promoted as an island classic is known as a bean crock, or bean jar – a ribsticking casserole of pork, beans and onions. You may also come across black butter, which, despite its name, contains no dairy products at all. Instead, it's a long-brewed mixture of apples, sugar, lemons and cider, flavoured with liquorice. Try it spread on a slice of *gâche* (see above).

DRINKS

The Normans introduced cider to the islands, but today beer is more popular. The Channel Islands also produce their own version of a cream liqueur, rather like Baileys. You may find an apple brandy on Jersey, made at Le Mare Vineyards. Local beers you will likely see everywhere include Guernsey Brewery ales and Mary Ann from Jersey. Randalls no longer brews its own beer, but imports real ale and owns many Channel Island pubs. You can find excellent pubs all over the islands.

Shopping

The Channel Islands market themselves as an inexpensive destination because duties are low and there is no VAT. Freight costs can erode this advantage and you should take advice before arranging for purchases to be shipped directly to the UK – you may end up having to pay VAT when they pass through customs. Also, don't forget that non-EU customs restrictions apply to any luxury purchased in the Channel Islands that you take back to the UK. Alcohol and tobacco are cheap, but savings on other goods are not always as great as you might expect. Prices vary significantly from one outlet to another, and from island to island, so shop around.

ST PETER PORT

St Peter Port has the best shopping centres and streets in Guernsey, but there are good (and sometimes cheaper) shops elsewhere on the island, such as The Bridge at St Sampson. The Old Quarter in St Peter Port is good for antiques, while the streets around Victoria Road make a good starting point for a shopping spree.

PERFUME & COSMETICS

St Peter Port is full of perfumeries with expensive, named brands offered – everything from Estèe Launder to Chanel. There are also a few smaller, chemist-style outlets that offer less expensive options.

FLOWERS & BULBS

Send a bouquet of freesias or roses to someone at home – all you have to do is fill in an address form and pay up. Most florists will advise you on which flowers to choose and how best to have them delivered. Bulbs of the Guernsey Lily, or nerine, can be bought at St Peter's Garden Centre.

PHILATELY, ANTIQUES & BOOKS

To buy commemorative issues, visit the main post offices in St Peter Port, where large displays of stamps can be seen. Bygone-hunters should

⬤ *Browsing in the Old Guernsey Market*

head for Mill Street and Mansell Street in St Peter Port's old quarter, which is full of galleries and antique shops. The Guernsey Press Shop in St Peter Port has a good selection of books specifically about the Channel Islands.

ISLAND CRAFTS

For a one-stop centre where you can do all of your souvenir buying in one go, your best bet is to head for Guernsey's Oatlands Craft Centre in St Sampson in the north. You will also have the opportunity to watch local craftspeople at work at a number of different traditional industries.

JEWELLERY

Some of the largest jewellery showrooms on Guernsey are in St Peter Port (see pages 20–25). Guernsey silverware makes charming, portable presents for christenings and silver weddings.

Look out for 'ormer shell' jewellery (see page 99 for more information on this rare mollusc) and items made from tiny spoons or Guernsey milkcans. Check the workshops of Catherine Best (the Old Mill, St Martin), a leading designer of modern jewellery, and Bruce Russell (Le Gron, St Saviour). Also head for the Oatlands Craft Centre, in St Sampson, as detailed above. Note that Channel Island gold and silver is not subject to the same rigorous assay and hallmarking process as it is in the UK. Any 'guarantee' offered with jewellery generally refers to the quality of workmanship, rather than any intrinsic value.

KNITWEAR

A real Channel Island sweater makes an excellent buy. Jerseys come in many shapes, colours and styles, but a classic Guernsey is instantly recognisable. Nelson spotted the potential of this warm, hardwearing fisherman's garment and recommended it for the British navy. Stylish for both men and women, the oiled wool is specially stitched, twisted and seamed to repel water.

Traditional, hand-finished Guernseys are produced at Le Tricoteur, which has a factory shop at Perelle Bay. Other outlets with good ranges of knitwear include The Guernsey Shop, St Peter Port, and Sheep's Clothing (aka Guernsey Woollens – you can find several branches on Guernsey, Jersey and Sark). For a sweater with a difference, try an Alderney, sold at Alderney's Channel Jumper shop near Braye Harbour.

Kids

Guernsey, Herm, Sark and Alderney welcome kids, but remember that the islands enjoy a leisurely way of life – the term 'rushing about' is not in the usual vocabulary. Be aware that children won't necessarily find lively attractions such as theme parks and fairs. They will find lots of sporting activities, however, such as swimming, go-karting, horse riding and tennis, and fun holiday pursuits such as beachcombing. Guernsey, Herm, Sark and Alderney are also full of interest for kids who take a shine to history and archaeology.

TOP ACTIVITIES
Guernsey

Guernsey's coastal fortresses and museums make special efforts to appeal to all ages. Don't miss ancient **Castle Cornet** (page 20), especially when the noonday gun is fired, and the **shipwreck museum** in Fort Grey (page 34). **Sausmarez Manor** (page 40) offers a miniature railway, pets, putting and a scrambly castle.

The National Trust's **Folk Museum at Saumarez Park** (page 29) and the **Victorian shop** at 26 Cornet Street, St Peter Port, both have child-

◑ *Passing time on the beach*

appeal. The **Beau Séjour Centre** offers plenty of sports and a fine swimming pool, plus a cinema and special summer events. Catch the pretty **Little Chapel**, a child-proportioned shrine covered with mosaics of shells and pottery (page 39). **The Track**, just outside St Peter Port, offers go-karting.

Herm

The Lilliputian scale of car-free Herm, with its flattish terrain and lovely beaches, is ideal for very young children who require little organised entertainment. Shrimping and shell-collecting, or building sandcastles, are its main pursuits.

Sark

Many children love the quaint, Toytown atmosphere of Sark. While older children will enjoy racing around the island on bikes, younger ones may prefer the gentler pace of a horsedrawn cart. Worth a try are the model railway exhibition, glass-blowing studio and pottery workshop.

● *Exploring Sark on wheels*

Alderney

Children will enjoy fortress-finding or visiting the lighthouse here. Most exciting for imaginative youngsters is the Elizabethan warship wrecked off Alderney's north-east coast. Take them to see the finds on display in Alderney museum and in the Glacis headquarters (better known as The Shed) at Braye Harbour, and find out about the salvage operation.

Beachcombing

Remember those childhood seaside holidays full of rock pools and sandcastles? Guernsey's beaches are the perfect place to relive those simple, old-fashioned pleasures. Armed with buckets, spades and shrimping nets, children can have days of cost-free fun. Tidal seawater pools, such as that at La Valette in St Peter Port, or the Venus Pool on Sark, offer sheltered bathing for older children.

Excursions

Guernsey offers the best choice of island-hopping destinations, with Herm and Sark just offshore, and Alderney within easy reach. Jersey is a good excursion too, while France seems a mere stone's throw away. Channel Island waters can be very choppy, especially round Sark, so choose a calm day.

If you're planning a visit to Alderney, a trip in one of Aurigny's tiny canary-coloured Trislander planes is a real adventure for kids. Look out for Joey, the star of the fleet with the red nose and big eyes.

Events

The colourful parades of the **Battle of Flowers** are irresistible if you're on Guernsey in mid-August. In July, catch Guernsey's **Viaer Marchi** – a traditional open-air market at Saumarez Park. The smaller islands have summer carnivals and shows too. Alderney holds an autumn juggling festival, and in Alderney Week (August) there's masses of fun – fancy dress parades, children's races and tug-of-war contests, with bonfires and fireworks to follow.

Festival & events

Guernsey and the islands, especially Sark and Alderney, love festivals, carnival and special events, and are host to many throughout the year. Some of the biggest annual events are listed below, although you'll find many other things going on.

Precise dates vary from year to year, so check with the tourist office. Most are geared to the main holiday season (Easter to October). Besides the normal public holidays observed in the UK, the Channel Islands commemorate Liberation Day (9 May – the end of German occupation) and Remembrance Sunday (mid-November) with fervour. Alderney takes its August bank holiday on the first Monday of the month, as part of its Alderney Week celebrations.

GUERNSEY
- Viaer Marchi (July): an old-time market in Saumarez Park
- Town Carnival (July): parades and events in St Peter Port
- Battle of Flowers (August): a less lavish version of Jersey's big do
- Guernsey Festival (October): arts events all over the island

SARK
- Midsummer Show (June): flower and produce stalls
- Water Carnival (July): raft races and jolly japes in Le Creux Harbour
- Autumn Show (August): agricultural livestock and produce
- Horse Show (September): horse and carriage contest and races

ALDERNEY
- Milk-a-Punch Sunday (May): free milk and rum cocktails dispensed by local pubs
- Alderney Week (August): classic carnival scenes with off-beat extras
- Juggling Festival (September)
- Annual Sprint and Hillclimb (September)
- Angling Festival (October)

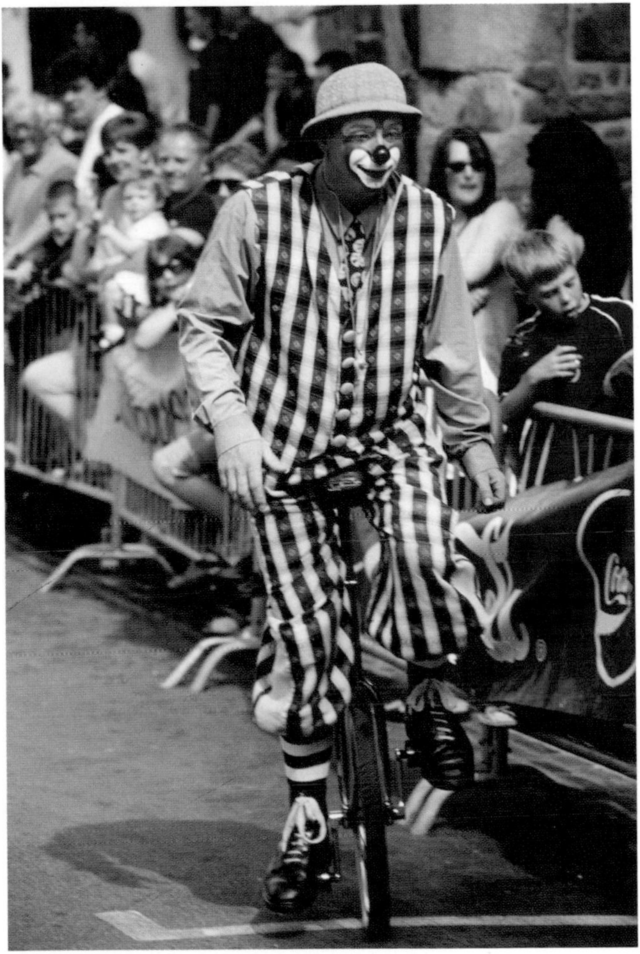

Don’t miss the fun of carnival, St Peter Port in July

Sports & activities

Guernsey offers a wide range of organised sports facilities. The Beau Séjour in St Peter Port is the largest and provides one-stop fitness in the form of swimming pools, tennis and squash courts. There's a surprising amount of sporting activity on Alderney. Its most famous resident, the late John Arlott, and its current cricket star, Ian Botham, generate a keen interest in the crack of leather on willow.

◯ *Riding the surf*

Other active passions among its residents include homing pigeons, a ladies darts league, bell-ringing, bowls and badminton, diving, clay pigeon shooting, motor sports and aviation. Visitors are always welcome to join in. Predictably, the smallest islands expect you to make your own arrangements for keeping in shape. With walking on Herm or cycling on Sark the only practical ways to explore, that isn't too difficult. These activities are immensely popular on the other islands too; excellent walking and cycling booklets and maps are available from the tourist offices containing suggested routes and information.

WATER SPORTS

With all that sea on the doorstep, it's hardly surprising that there's plenty for waterbabies to do. Windsurfing enthusiasts should head to Cobo and L'Ancresse Bays on Guernsey for tuition or equipment. Diving is an attractive proposition in the clear waters around the Channel Islands, but you should take advice about currents. Wreck diving is a speciality. There is a diving centre in Havelet Bay on Guernsey.

For novices, surfing here should probably remain a spectator sport, but experienced surfers may like to pit their skill against the Atlantic breakers of Vazon Bay in Guernsey. Other watery activities include canoeing, rowing, pedalos, jet-skiing, parascending, speedboating and 'banana boats' – available from the main water sports centre at Havelet Bay on Guernsey.

SAILING

The ritzy marinas around the Channel Islands soon tell you these waters represent nirvana for many yachtsfolk. If you're not lucky enough to own some ocean-going gin palace, you can always hire one, skippered or bareboat.

FISHING

Channel Island waters attract a wide range of species of fish. Sea and wreck-fishing boats can also be chartered on most of the islands. Ask at the tourist office for further details.

GOLF

The enthusiasm for harrying small white balls into tiny holes knows no bounds on the Channel Islands. So many courses have sprung up that it's surprising they don't overlap. Egged on by resident golfing millionaires, Guernsey now has a number of greens, not counting numerous pitch-and-putt and mini-golf courses. Guernsey's most popular golf club is the Royal Guernsey at L'Ancresse Bay. Two hotel-based courses at La Grande Mare, Vazon Bay, and St Pierre Park (designed by Tony Jacklin) cater for the overspill. Sausmarez Manor has an enjoyable nine-hole pitch-and-putt course in its beautiful grounds. Alderney also has a challenging nine-hole course, with low green fees.

HORSE RIDING

Numerous schools on Guernsey offer tuition and escorted hacking. Tourist offices can supply lists of riding schools and racing fixtures.

RACQUET SPORTS

Tennis, squash and badminton courts can be hired at the main sports complexes. Alderney also has a tennis club.

MOTOR SPORTS

Sand-racing, hillclimbing, rallies and motocross events are organised at various times throughout the year on Guernsey. The Tourist Information Office on North Esplanade, St Peter Port, is the best place to find out what's happening (☎ 01481 723 552).

BOWLS

Lawn bowls can be played in several locations on Guernsey, including outdoor bowls at Beau Séjour, and indoors at Hougue du Pommier and Fort Regent.

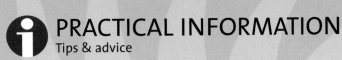

PRACTICAL INFORMATION
Tips & advice

Preparing to go

GETTING THERE

By far the best way to visit Guernsey is as part of an inclusive package, although travelling independently by booking a flight and accommodation is popular too. Guernsey is well served by airlines, and there are regular flights from airports in the UK, including Birmingham, London Gatwick and Stansted, Exeter, Manchester and Norwich. Travelling by sea to Jersey is easy from Poole, Portsmouth and Weymouth. For information on tour operators featuring Guernsey visit ⓦ www.abta.com.

BEFORE YOU LEAVE

Holidays should be about fun and relaxation, so avoid last-minute panics and stress by making your preparations well in advance. You do not need inoculations to travel to Guernsey, Herm, Sark or Alderney, but it is worth checking that you and your family are up-to-date with the basics, such as tetanus. If you take prescription medicines, make sure you have enough to last the whole trip. Consider packing a small first-aid kit containing plasters, antiseptic cream, travel sickness pills, insect repellent and/or bite-relief cream, upset stomach remedies and painkillers. Take plenty of sunscreen – Guernsey and the islands can get very hot in high summer. Remember, too, to make arrangements for the care of your pets while you are away.

DOCUMENTS

The most important documents you will need are your tickets and passport, plus your driving licence if you are planning to take your car or hire one while on Guernsey. If you plan to have more than one driver of the vehicle make sure that they, too, have their driving licence. Passports are not needed by UK citizens for travel to the Channel Islands, however you will want them if you are thinking of an excursion to France. Remember photo ID will be required by your airline and if you need medical assistance. Make sure that your passports are up-to-date and have at least three months left to run. All children, including newborn babies, need their own passport now. It generally takes at least three weeks to process a passport renewal. This can be longer in the run-up to the summer months. Contact the **Passport Agency** for the latest information on how to renew your passport and the processing times involved (❶ 0870 521 0410 Ⓦ www.ukpa.gov.uk).

Always check the details on your travel tickets well before your departure, ensuring that the timings and dates are correct.

MONEY

Although Guernsey and the islands have their own notes and coins, UK currency is legal tender in the Channel Islands so you do not need to worry about currency exchange or travellers' cheques. However, you should make sure that your credit, charge and debit cards are up-to-date – you do not want them to expire mid holiday – and that your credit limit is sufficient to allow you to make those holiday purchases. Your bank or card company will assist you . Don't forget, too, to check your PIN numbers in case you haven't used them for a while – you may want to draw money from cash dispensers while you are away (but do not draw out too much, as Channel Islands currency will not be accepted back in the UK). Remember there are no cash dispensers on the smaller islands.

INSURANCE

Do you have adequate cover for your holiday? Check that your policy covers you adequately for loss of possessions and valuables, for activities you might want to try – such as scuba diving, horse-riding, or water sports – and for emergency medical and dental treatment, including flights home if required. You do not need an EHIC medical card (it has replaced the E111) but you do need proof of UK citizenship to obtain treatment. For further information, telephone EHIC enquiries line (❶ 0845 605 0707) or visit the Department of Health website (Ⓦ www.dh.gov.uk).

CLIMATE

Guernsey, Herm, Sark and Alderney enjoy long, hot summer days. The winters are mild. Despite a deceptive sea breeze, the air is clear and the ultra-violet is strong. Be sure to cover up and slap on the sun cream when it becomes particularly hot.

SECURITY

Take sensible precautions to protect your house being burgled while you are away:

- Cancel milk, newspapers and other regular deliveries so it does not pile up on the doorstep.
- Let the postman know where to leave parcels and bulky mail that will not go through your letterbox – ideally with a next-door neighbour.
- If possible, arrange for a friend or neighbour to visit regularly, closing and opening curtains, and switching lights on and off, or consider buying timing devices that switch lights and radios on and off.
- Let Neighbourhood Watch representatives know that you will be away so that they can keep an eye on your home.
- If you have a burglar alarm, make sure that it is serviced and working properly and is switched on when you leave (you may find that your insurance policy requires this). Ensure that a neighbour is able to gain access to the alarm if necessary to turn it off if it is set off accidentally.
- If you are leaving cars unattended, put them in a garage, if possible, and leave a key with a neighbour in case the alarm goes off.

AIRPORT PARKING & ACCOMMODATION

If you intend to park your car while you are away, or stay the night at an airport hotel before or after your flight, you should book well ahead to take advantage of discounts or cheap off-airport parking. Airport accommodation gets booked up several weeks in advance, especially during the height of the holiday season. Check whether the hotel offers free parking for the duration of the holiday – often the savings made on parking costs can make the accommodation price significantly more attractive.

BAGGAGE ALLOWANCE

Baggage allowances vary according to the airline, destination and the
class of travel, but 20 kg (44 lb) per person is the norm for luggage that
is carried in the hold (it usually tells you what the weight limit is on
your ticket); in addition you are allowed one item of cabin baggage
weighing no more than 5 kg (11 lb), and measuring 46 by 30 by 23 cm
(18 by 12 by 9 inches). You can carry your duty-free purchases, umbrella,
handbag, coat, camera, etc as hand baggage. Large items – surfboards,
golf-clubs, collapsible wheelchairs and pushchairs – are usually charged
as extras and it is a good idea to let the airline know in advance that
you want to bring these.

You should also consider packing the following:

- **Checklist of UK prices** For items you may want to buy while you are
  on holiday. Because of low taxation and the absence of VAT, cameras,
  electronic goods, clothing, perfumes, cigarettes, alcohol and jewellery
  can be cheaper than in other parts of Europe.
- **Camera**
- **Driving licence** You will need this to hire a car (even if you've
  prebooked one) or a moped. Photocopies of your licence are not
  accepted on the islands.
- **Photo ID and/or passport** The latter if you think you may be tempted
  by the idea of hopping over to France for the day.
- **Sensible footwear** You're bound to want to do some walking at some
  point, if only to walk around St Peter Port's steep cobbles.
- **Wet weather gear** Sadly, sunshine cannot be guaranteed.
- **Warm sweater** But save space in your suitcase to take home a real
  Channel Island Jersey or Guernsey.
- **Pocket binoculars** And perhaps a field guide to birds or wildflowers,
  if you are a keen nature buff.
- **National Trust card** If you have one – both Guernsey and neighbour-
  ing Jersey have affiliated NT branches that allow UK members free
  access to their properties.

- **Bucket and spade, snorkelling gear** For sandcastle architects of all ages and swimmers.
- **For local holiday reading** You may be interested in Jenny Wood's account of life on Herm as the Tenant's wife, or the enthusiastic books about Jersey written by John Nettles on the making of the 1980s *Bergerac* TV series. Classics also include Compton Mackenzie's novel *Fairy Gold*, based on Jethou, and Victor Hugo's *Toilers of the Sea*, set in Guernsey.

CHECK-IN, PASSPORT CONTROL & CUSTOMS

First-time travellers can often find airport security intimidating, but it is all very easy, really. If you are travelling from a large airport, check which terminal before you leave home.

- Check-in desks usually open two hours before the flight is due to depart. Arrive early for the best choice of seats.
- Look for your flight number on the TV monitors in the check-in area, and find the relevant check-in desk. Your tickets will be checked and your luggage labelled. Take your boarding card and go to the departure gate, where your boarding pass will be checked. There are no passport controls for flights to the Channel Islands, but you will go through a security check, during which your hand luggage will be X-rayed.
- In the departure area, you can shop and relax, but watch the monitors that tell you when your flight is ready to board – usually about 30 minutes before take-off. Go to the departure gate shown on the monitor and follow the instructions given to you by the airline staff.

Guernsey, as with all the Channel Islands, is not a full member of the European Union, and allowances are less generous than those between other member states. You may take only 200 cigarettes, a litre of spirits, 60ml perfume or £145 worth of other goods including gifts and souvenirs either into the Channel Islands or back to the UK.

During your stay

BEACHES

Guernsey, as with Herm, Sark and Alderney, is surrounded by some of the swiftest currents and highest tides in the world. West coast beaches are exposed to powerful Atlantic breakers – wonderful for experienced surfers, but unsuitable for weak swimmers. Never try to cross a causeway or explore sea caves without checking the tide tables and pay attention to warning signs. Do not swim if red flags are flying. Lifeguards are posted on some of the more popular beaches in summer. Remember red flag means dangerous conditions and no swimming; yellow means only good swimmers should take to the water, and a green flag indicates that conditions are safe.

CHILDREN'S ACTIVITIES

Most Guernsey residents will welcome children and there is plenty for them to do. There are attractions and sporting activities aimed at children, and the many fortifications scattered all over the island make tempting places for children to play and hide. Do remember, however, that some castles and ruins are derelict and may be dangerous to explore. Guernsey and its islands are relatively safe and children should come to no harm.

TOURIST INFORMATION

Guernsey's main tourist office is at the Guernsey Information Centre, North Esplanade, St Peter Port (☎ 1481 723 552). For Sark, visit the Sark Tourist Information Centre on Harbour Hill (☎ 1481 832 345). The Alderney Tourism Information Centre is in Victoria Street (☎ 1481 823 737). For Herm contact the Herm Island Administration Office (☎ 1481 722 377).

CURRENCY

Sterling is acceptable in Guernsey, Herm, Sark and Alderney, so you don't need to change any money. The Bailiwicks of Guernsey issue their own coins and banknotes, but these are not legal tender in the UK. Travellers'

cheques, UK cheques backed by a banker's card and major credit cards are all widely accepted methods of payment. There are no cash dispensers on the smaller islands.

ELECTRICITY

Guernsey has the same voltage as the UK, 240 volts AC, and uses British style three-pin sockets, so taking electrical items with you and using them won't present a problem.

GETTING AROUND

Car hire and driving

Hiring a car A hired car is the most popular way to explore Guernsey and Alderney, although remember that no cars are allowed on Sark or Herm. Rental rates are very reasonable. Choose the smallest car you think you can tolerate, because the lanes are too narrow for large vehicles, and are often lined by unforgiving granite walls or ditches. Locals are surprisingly tolerant of bewildered tourists blundering round their lanes. Remember that you must have a valid driving licence with no endorsements for dangerous or drunken driving in the last five years, and you must be aged 20 years and over.

Designated drivers If you think you may be over the limit after a night out on Guernsey and don't want to drive, call 'The Bike'. A sober chauffeur will appear on a moped that will neatly fold up in your car boot and you can thus be transported safely back to your hotel without risking your licence.

Speed limits The maximum speed limit is 55 kph (35 mph) on Guernsey, and 65 kph (40 mph) on Jersey. In towns it is 40 kph (25 mph) and on Green Lanes (extremely narrow roads with ditches or granite walls on either side) it is only 25 kph (15 mph).

Rules of the road Remember to drive on the left. A yellow line across a minor road means STOP. You must give way to traffic on the major road. Yellow arrows painted on the road warn of an approaching stop line, while a single yellow line along the side of the road means no parking at any time. A yellow box painted at a junction indicates a 'filter in turn' system. This simply means that all approach roads have equal priority, so you take it in turns with cars from other directions. Remember drink-driving penalties are strict.

Roads Road surfaces are good and road markings are clear, but be aware that some roads, known as Green Lanes, have a 25 kph (15 mph) speed limit – they are very narrow and have ditches on either side. They may also have granite walls either side that can leave a nasty dent in the side of your car if driving recklessly – a good reason not to exceed the limit.

Petrol Petrol is very cheap and a tankful goes a long way. Don't buy more than £5 worth at a time, as most rental firms expect you to take the car back empty.

Parking In Guernsey, all public parking is free (except at the airport), but you must use a parking clock in a disc zone, or you can expect to get a ticket. The disc system operates in St Anne on Alderney too. Long-stay parking places are in great demand in St Peter Port. If you want to leave your car for a whole day (while you visit another island, perhaps) try the 'park-and-ride' system that operates from Footes Road outside the town. More information is available from the Tourist Information Office on North Esplanade, or on Alderney centre in Victoria Street.

Public transport

Guernsey Has the highest proportion of motor vehicles per head of population in the world, with Jersey second. Needless to say, there are jams in the busier parts of the island, but it's surprising how quickly traffic disperses on all those tiny lanes. If you don't care to drive, buses operate along the main roads, and you can always hire a bike. Guernsey also has a splendid network of 'Green Lane' footpaths and coastal trails that take you through gorgeous scenery away from cars and madding crowds. The tourist offices produce excellent, clear walks leaflets which avoid busy roads as far as possible. The cliff path along the south coast on Guernsey takes you past the best of the islands' scenery.

Alderney An organised excursion is by far the easiest way to see something of the island on a brief visit. In high season, excursion coaches and minibuses operate daily from St Anne. You can also see most of Alderney on much cheaper scheduled bus services, or hire a bike, moped or car.

Herm You can easily walk round traffic-free Herm in two hours, and good beaches lie within as little as ten minutes' walk from the harbour. Most of the interior of the island consists of gentle countryside criss-crossed by easy paths. There are a few steeper paths with steps around the southern cliffs. Mini-tractors are available to carry heavy bags to and from the boats.

Sark Car-free Sark is larger and more hilly, with steep cliffs plunging down to cove beaches. Walking is the only way to explore the whole island in detail, but this takes longer than a day, hence the popularity of the bicycle on Sark. Several outlets hire bikes in the village (at least one stays open all year), but it's still advisable to book in advance through the ferry company in summer. Placid, well-groomed Shire horses await the ferry boats in summer, ready to take passengers on gentle jaunts round the island, usually including a spectacular crossing of La Coupée, a precipitous causeway just wide enough for the cartwheels. One carriage takes up to ten passengers. They're popular, so it's best to book ahead in summer. This can be done on an organised excursion, or ask the Isle of Sark Shipping company for a voucher when you buy your ticket.

Bus services Guernsey and Alderney have good bus systems, though services are less frequent off season, in the evenings, and on Sunday. An Explorer ticket lets you hop on and off as much as you like. Most services radiate from Guernsey's capital, St Peter Port and Alderney's St Anne. Timetables are available at main bus stations. Frequent services go from the main towns to the airports. Buses cost 50 pence per journey and are very comfortable. All have access for those with disabilities.

Taxis Taxi ranks can be found in St Peter Port and at the airport. Be aware that there are different tariffs applied for day and night hire and on public holidays. Extra charges may be charged for waiting time. Many taxi firms operate taxis with easy wheelchair access.

Ferries Travel between Guernsey and mainline UK, the islands of Alderney, Sark and Herm, and Jersey and France, is easy from St Peter Port. Try **Condor Ferries** (☏ 0845 345 2000 ⓦ www.condorferries.com).

HEALTH MATTERS

The UK National Health Service does not operate in Guernsey and all doctors, dentists and opticians are in private practice. But, as the UK has reciprocal health arrangements, British visitors enjoy free medical treatment while they are on the islands. Not all costs are covered, however, and it is advisable to take out health insurance. Urgent dental problems, such as a sudden abscess, may be treated as medical emergencies.

There is no need to take any forms with you, such as an EHIC medical card (which has replaced the E111 form), but you do need to provide proof of identity and UK citizenships to obtain treatment (for eg. a driving licence). Prescription charges are much lower than in the UK, but take with you any medicines you need regularly. For further information contact the **Board of Health** on Guernsey (📞 01481 725 241).

CLINICS

Guernsey The A & E Department is at the **Princess Elizabeth Hospital**. **The Pier Steps Surgery** runs a free morning clinic (📍 High Street, St Peter Port; basement of Boots 📞 01481 711 237 🕐 Open Mon–Sat). For minor holiday ailments, the **Pollet Pharmacy**, in central St Peter Port, is very helpful. **Sark** Go to the **Medical Centre** (📍 Seigneurie Road 📞 01481 832 045). Try not to get toothache on Sark or Herm – there is no dentist. **Alderney** Go to the **Island Medical Centre** (📍 Ollivier Street 📞 01481 822 077) or **Dental Practice** (📍 Venelles du Milieu 📞 01481 823 131).

PERSONAL COMFORT & SECURITY

Crime prevention Crime (especially personal violence or street theft) is rare in the Bailiwick of Guernsey. Even so, there are a few things to watch out for: for example, even if the islanders themselves don't always lock their doors, it makes sense for visitors to do so. Don't leave temptation in anyone's way and you are unlikely to suffer any losses.

Lost property Report any loss or theft to your holiday representative. If an insurance claim is to be made you must report a theft within 24 hours to the police. Call the lost property office in Guernsey (📞 01481 725 111). Remember to also notify your bank or credit card company as quickly

as possible if you lose your cheque book, debit or credit cards.

Police Traffic congestion is a serious problem on Guernsey, which has narrow lanes and blind bends, often lined with granite walls, and no footpaths. Great care is needed on the roads at all times. For emergencies call ❶ 999 for police, fire, ambulance or coastal rescue services.

POST OFFICES
Guernsey's pillar boxes are blue. You must use the correct stamps on any post mailed from the islands. For Guernsey, Sark or Herm use Guernsey stamps; for Alderney either Guernsey or Alderney stamps can be used; and if visiting Jersey, mail must carry Jersey stamps (postal systems in Guernsey and Jersey are not interchangeable). The central post offices and museums in Guernsey have interesting displays of local stamps, which illustrate many aspects of island life and history.

TELEPHONES
Channel Island telecom services are modern, efficient and relatively inexpensive. Public call boxes (mostly yellow, but green on Sark) are widespread, and use the same STD codes as the UK. In Guernsey some telephone boxes take 10, 20 or 50p coins as well as cards. Phone cards are sold in newsagents and post offices.

TIME DIFFERENCES
There is no time difference between the Channel Islands and the UK.

WEIGHTS & MEASUREMENTS
Guernsey operates the metric system as in the UK.

TELEPHONING THE CHANNEL ISLANDS
The dialling code for Guernsey, Herm, Sark and Alderney is ❶ 01481. The dialling code for Jersey is ❶ 01534.

INDEX

A

Alderney 8, 10, 13, 17, 45, 54–60, 65, 104, 107, 108, 111, 112, 120, 121
art galleries 23, 34

B

Bailiwick of Guernsey Tapestry 20
Battle of Flowers 94, 107, 108
beaches 119
    Alderney 59, 65
    Bailiwick beach tour 62–5
    Guernsey 18, 30, 62–4, 107
    Herm 13, 46, 65
    Jersey 13, 94
    Sark 51, 65, 107
'The Bike' 120
birdwatching 13, 49, 56–7, 86, 96
boat trips 49, 56
Bouley Bay 88
bowls 112
Brecqhou 13, 53
Bronze Age relics 18, 39
Burhou Island 57

C

Castel 10, 30–2
castles and fortresses
    Alderney 13, 17, 56
    Guernsey 17–18, 20, 26, 34, 63, 105
    Jersey 68, 69, 71, 88, 90
causeways 10, 35, 119
children 29, 30, 81, 94, 105–7, 119
churches and chapels
    Alderney 57
    Guernsey 16, 17, 20, 39
    Herm 42, 43
    Jersey 77, 78, 80
crafts 29, 34, 40, 82, 106
    jewellery 29, 30, 36, 78, 95, 104
    knitwear 29, 30, 64, 104
    pottery 29, 40, 62, 80, 89, 95, 106
    woodcraft 32, 89
currency 119–20

D

designated drivers 120
Dinard 75
diving 26, 111
dolmens 26, 43

E

excursions 61–96, 107

F

festival and events 107, 108
fishing 26, 88, 111
flowers and bulbs 27, 88, 89, 102
food and drink 46, 98–101
Forest 10, 36–41

G

Geoffrey's Leap 88
German Occupation Museum 18, 36
German Underground Hospitals 39, 76, 78
Glass Church 77, 80
go-karting 26
gold and silversmiths 30
golf 112
Gorey Village 89
Gran'mère du Chimquière 18, 39

H

Hammond Memorial 56
Hauteville House 20, 23
Herm 8, 10, 12, 13, 42–7, 49, 65, 106, 111, 118, 120, 122
horse riding 112
Hugo, Victor 20, 23, 62

J

Jersey 8, 13, 107
    northern tour 86–93
    St Helier 68–75
    St Ouen 94–6
    southern tour 76–85
Jethou 13, 43, 118

L

La Coupée 18, 49, 50
La Mare Vineyards 86, 90, 101
La Pierre aux Rats 43
La Seigneurie 49, 50
La Vallette Underground Military
    Museum 18, 23
L'Ancresse Common 26
Langtry, Lillie 77
lavender 78
Le Manoir 43
Les Etacs Rocks 56–7
lighthouses 57, 63, 107
Lihou 8, 10, 35, 63
L'ile Agois 86
Little Chapel 38, 39, 105
Little Sark 18, 49, 50, 51, 65
Living Legend 81

M

marinas 10, 13, 26, 64, 111
markets 25, 107
Martello towers 17, 33, 34, 96
Mont St Michel 75
motor sports 112
museums
    Alderney 56, 58, 107
    Guernsey 17, 18, 20, 23, 29, 34, 36,
        63, 105
    Jersey 68–9, 71, 76, 78, 80, 82, 89, 94
    Sark 50

N

nature reserves 55, 89
neolithic sites 26, 43, 80–1

O

Occupation Tapestry 71, 73
ormers 99, 104

P

pearls 95
prehistoric sites 86

R

racquet sports 112
Rozel 88

S

sailing 111
St Andrew 10, 36–41
St Brelade 76
St Helier 68–75
St Malo 75
St Martin 10, 36–41
St Martin's Church 16, 17, 18, 39
St Peter Port 8, 10, 17, 18, 20–5, 102,
    103, 104, 105, 110
St Peter in the Wood 10, 33–5
St Sampson 10, 26–9, 104
St Saviour 10, 30–2
Sark 8, 10, 11, 13, 18, 44, 48–53, 65, 106,
    107, 108, 111, 120, 122
Saumarez Park 28, 29, 107
Sausmarez Manor 11, 40, 41, 105
Shell Beach 46, 65
shopping 8, 25, 55, 102–4
    markets 25, 107
silver mines 51
snorkelling 63
surfing 30, 64, 94, 111
swimming 10, 26, 36, 107

T

tax 8, 11, 55, 102
Torteval 10, 33–5

V

Vale 10, 26–9

W / Z

walking 34, 86, 94, 111
water sports 76, 111
windsurfing 26, 111
World War II 18, 23, 36, 39, 49, 50, 71,
    76, 81, 98, 108
zoo 88, 90

ACKNOWLEDGEMENTS

We would like to thank all the photographers, picture libraries and organisations for the loan of the photographs reproduced in this book, to whom copyright in the photograph belongs:
Fiona Adams (page 106); J Allan Cash (page 51);
De Wildenberg (page 41); Guernsey Tourist Board (pages 58, 71, 76, 82, 87);
Jersey Tourism (pages 69, 73, 74, 77, 79, 80, 81, 82, 85, 87, 88, 95, 97, 100, 110);
Jupiter Images Corporation (pages 113, 125); Sunworld (page 105); Thomas Cook Tour Operations Ltd (page 48); VisitGuernsey (pages 1, 5, 9, 12, 16, 19, 21, 27, 28, 31, 33, 37, 38, 39, 42, 46, 53, 54, 57, 58, 61, 63, 91, 103, 109).

We would also like to thank the following for their contribution to this series:
John Woodcock (map and symbols artwork);
Katie Greenwood (picture research);
Patricia Baker, Rachel Carter, Judith Chamberlain-Webber, Nicky Falkof, Nicky Gyopari, Stephanie Horner, Robin Pridy (editorial support);
Christine Engert, Suzie Johanson, Richard Lloyd, Richard Peters, Alistair Plumb, Jane Prior, Barbara Theisen, Ginny Zeal, Barbara Zuñiga (design support).

Send your thoughts to
books@thomascook.com

- Found a beach bar, peaceful stretch of sand or must-see sight that we don't feature?
- Like to tip us off about any information that needs a little updating?
- Want to tell us what you love about this handy, little guidebook and more importantly how we can make it even handier?

Then here's your chance to tell all! Send us ideas, discoveries and recommendations today and then look out for your valuable input in the next edition of this title. And, as an extra 'thank you' from Thomas Cook Publishing, you'll be automatically entered into our exciting monthly prize draw.

Send an email to the above address or write to:
HotSpots Project Editor, Thomas Cook Publishing, PO Box 227, Unit 15/16, Coningsby Road, Peterborough PE3 8SB, UK.